THE LOTUS STILL BLOOMS

The
LOTUS
STILL BLOOMS

Sacred Buddhist Teachings
for the Western Mind

Joan Gattuso

JEREMY P. TARCHER/PENGUIN
a member of Penguin Group (USA) Inc.
New York

JEREMY P. TARCHER/PENGUIN
Published by the Penguin Group
Penguin Group (USA) Inc., 375 Hudson Street, New York, New York 10014,
USA · Penguin Group (Canada), 90 Eglinton Avenue East, Suite 700, Toronto,
Ontario M4P 2Y3, Canada (a division of Pearson Canada Inc.) · Penguin
Books Ltd, 80 Strand, London WC2R 0RL, England · Penguin Ireland,
25 St Stephen's Green, Dublin 2, Ireland (a division of Penguin Books Ltd) ·
Penguin Group (Australia), 250 Camberwell Road, Camberwell, Victoria 3124,
Australia (a division of Pearson Australia Group Pty Ltd) · Penguin Books
India Pvt Ltd, 11 Community Centre, Panchsheel Park, New Delhi–110 017,
India · Penguin Group (NZ), 67 Apollo Drive, Rosedale, North Shore 0632,
New Zealand (a division of Pearson New Zealand Ltd) · Penguin Books (South
Africa) (Pty) Ltd, 24 Sturdee Avenue, Rosebank, Johannesburg 2196, South Africa

Penguin Books Ltd, Registered Offices:
80 Strand, London WC2R 0RL, England

Most Tarcher/Penguin books are available at special quantity discounts
for bulk purchase for sales promotions, premiums, fund-raising, and
educational needs. Special books or book excerpts also can be created to
fit specific needs. For details, write Penguin Group (USA) Inc.
Special Markets, 375 Hudson Street, New York, NY 10014.

Library of Congress Cataloging-in-Publication Data

Gattuso, Joan M.
The lotus still blooms / Joan Gattuso.
p.   cm.
ISBN 978-1-58542-637-9
1. Religious life—Buddhism.   2. Buddhism—Doctrines.   I. Title.
BQ4302.G36   2008   2008018846
294.3—dc22

Printed in the United States of America
1   3   5   7   9   10   8   6   4   2

BOOK DESIGN BY AMANDA DEWEY

While the author has made every effort to provide accurate telephone
numbers and Internet addresses at the time of publication, neither the
publisher nor the author assumes any responsibility for errors, or for
changes that occur after publication. Further, the publisher does not have
any control over and does not assume any responsibility for author or
third-party websites or their content.

To His Holiness the Dalai Lama

Acknowledgments

With a sincere heart, I acknowledge and thank:

- My always loving and supportive husband, David Alexander.
- My brilliant and skillful agent, Anne Sibbald.
- Joel Fotinos and Sarah Litt of Jeremy P. Tarcher/Penguin for endless support and patience with all of my questions.
- My closest Buddhist teachers with whom I have studied—His Holiness the Dalai Lama, Sogal Rinpoche, Thich Nhat Hanh, Lama Chonam, Sangye Kandro and Robert Thurman, and the various Buddhist nuns and monks who have paused briefly on my path.
- My spiritual sojourner, Reverend Linda Spencer.
- The fellow Unity ministers with whom I walk—Reverends Sandra Hymel, Stan and Barbara Smith, Ric Schmacher, Joann Landreth, Suzanne Stover and Ron Stover.
- My precious lifelong friends Susan Miller Schwabe, Nancy Miller, Courtney Lang, Dr. Minner Bowers, Dr. Ileana Pina, Adrienne Gerspacher, Barbara Hill, Bob Javorski, Dr. Keith Jordan, John Broad, Ronn Liller, Karen Karsh, Peter Clancy, Dr. Jacqueline Rogers and Sandy Deck.

- My departed friend Georgia Drakes, who first introduced me to His Holiness the Dalai Lama.
- My family—my mom, who I am so grateful is still with us; my brother Jim and his wife, Vicki; Grady and his family; Sabrina and her family; and my precious and loving stepdaughters, Robyn, Lisa, and Julie and their families.
- My staff members, who are more like family than staff: Felicia Martinez, her three daughters, and Rudi Barnes.
- Last, but far from least, our three precious four-legged "daughters"—transplanted Hawaii kitty Petite Noir and Yorkies Honey and Tara, each of whom brings joy to every day we share.

Contents

All great religions have methods for overcoming suffering.
Buddhism is just one example.

—HIS HOLINESS THE DALAI LAMA

Introduction

W HILE I WAS ON A BOOK TOUR in Los Angeles, a totally unexpected
and life-expanding event began to unfold. I had a free afternoon
in which my childhood friend Ginna, then the chef at Deepak Chopra's
healing center, was coming to fetch me for the day. She was temporarily
on leave from the healing center, living in the Los Angeles area and working as the personal chef for an action-movie hero while he was getting in
shape for his upcoming movie.

Ginna offered me a choice: Would I prefer to go to his movie set, or
would I like to see his home in Bel Air? I instantly chose his home, a
spontaneous decision for which I remain grateful to this day.

The Bel Air area is most luxurious, lined with manicured estates. We
pulled through the gates of a grand home. Upon entering we were greeted
in the kitchen by the young live-in girlfriend, who appeared to be a little
upset. Ginna, multitalented artist, chef, earth-mother goddess personified, said she needed to talk with the young woman. Did I mind being
alone for a while? Of course I told Ginna I did not. It was fascinating
sitting in the kitchen observing the famous movie star's domestic life
filled with two nannies, a cook, a helper and a chauffeur—all in the
kitchen at the same time. I took in a very animated conversation in the

midst of the unpacked groceries that were everywhere. Then the unexpected occurred.

Through the kitchen doorway two Tibetan monks in robes and wearing mala beads entered the kitchen. I immediately stood and bowed to them. They bowed to me, while my brain raced to comprehend this increasingly bizarre kitchen scene. The monks took seats opposite me at the kitchen table. We introduced ourselves. They were guests in the actor's home while they were studying English at UCLA. The older of the two barely understood English, while the younger was fairly fluent.

After only a few minutes the younger one asked innocently, "Do you want to come to my room?"

I was for a fraction of a second taken aback, not having received such an offer in many a year, let alone from a young Tibetan monk in saffron robes. "Okay, I guess so," I responded haltingly. This is how I met Lama Chonam, my most precious Buddhist friend.

We walked through the great rooms of the mansion and up the stairs to the second floor. When we reached his room, the young monk opened the door and we entered. It was more like a sanctuary than a bedroom. It consisted of a beautiful altar with many butter candles burning, artistic figures of the Buddha, and various Taras and bodhisattvas.

He placed two chairs near the altar, and we sat at a right angle to each other. In the depths of my being I knew this was a significant occurrence. He opened his heart to me that afternoon, telling me of his arduous escape from Tibet over the Himalayas and into Nepal. His tales were spellbinding. He was amazed that I had been studying with the Dalai Lama for several years and had married my Western spiritual education to my Tibetan practices. We sat together for two hours deeply engaged in conversation, like two lost friends who had finally found each other again after many years or lifetimes of being separated.

When it was time to go, he walked me to the car and said, "We must have very good karma together." Then he did an extraordinary thing for a monk. He reached out and hugged me, and I hugged him in return. "I have met many Americans," he said, "but I never have met anyone that I felt so connected to. It is like we are meeting again. And you came to this house so we could meet. We shall meet again."

And so we have, many times. He has taught Buddhism at my church, and as the years have gone by he has become a respected teacher in his own right within Buddhism.

Lama Chonam has the purest heart of anyone I personally know. And to think that on the day I thought I was to see a movie star's home, a Tibetan monk saw my heart and I saw his.

I share this tender story because it so solidified for me that it is possible to remain a minister of Christian metaphysics and also to incorporate the Buddhist teachings on my path. Meeting Lama Chonam was for me a Divine message saying, Yes, it can and does all weave together into a most meaningful whole.

MY JOURNEY IN BUDDHISM began many years earlier, in the autumn of 1991, when two life-altering events occurred for me. The first was surgery for uterine cancer, and the second was my first encounter with the teachings of Tibetan Buddhism and being with His Holiness the Dalai Lama.

This second event happened at Madison Square Garden in New York City, where I arrived in a wheelchair, just days out of surgery. Going to New York was one of those absolute knowings in life, where from my toes to my soul I just knew I had to go.

A friend in my congregation who was deeply attached to the people of India and Nepal, having adopted a child from each country, encouraged me to accompany her. I "knew" I was meant to go. The journey was undertaken much to my husband David's consternation, since it was so few days after major surgery. I went having no idea what to expect or how my life would be forever changed.

At that first encounter of the teachings my knowledge of Buddhism was minuscule. I had, however, been practicing a Buddhist contemplation technique known as Mindfulness Meditation for more than a dozen years. I simply listened to my inner urging to attend and went. In short order a long-slumbering Eastern soul—more aligned with Eastern thought and culture than Western—within me began to stir and awaken. From that day to this I have inquired, studied, practiced, traveled, retreated and now teach what I have learned and am learning.

I am not a Buddhist teacher and have no claims of being such. I have been a student of eternal truths and a teacher of spiritual principle for more than thirty years. In retrospect it seems logical that my initial awakening began with the Unity Church, of which I have been a minister for twenty-nine years. Unity is a nondenominational spiritual movement of churches that focuses on the emerging of the inner spirit and teaches one to seek to know and practice the eternal principles of truth. Unity is not about dogma or creed, but rather bringing forth, as Thoreau stated, "the inner splendor." Next my soul moved into the spiritual text *A Course in Miracles*, from its initial emergence into the spiritual culture of America in the 1970s. Today it is a popular tome containing eternal truths. As a student of these two paths I easily found points of agreement and fused both into my awakening consciousness. My friend Andrew Harvey, the twenty-first-century mystic, says, "All true spiritual teachings ultimately converge." They were converging in my soul.

I have studied Tibetan Buddhism since that first encounter with His Holiness the Dalai Lama in 1991. The spiritual disciplines I have learned on my path have become so much a part of me that I have begun to constantly have insights and realizations on the ultimate nature of reality. There is a point where *all* teachings converge and the common thread of truth can be seen. That is happening in my life, and I am endeavoring to share how that can occur with you in your life.

As the years passed, and my study of Tibetan Buddhism deepened, I began to see clearly this convergence of Buddhism, my Unity teachings, the teachings in *A Course in Miracles* and myriad teachings in other spiritual books. I was excited. I was on fire with the possibility of true awakening. I realized, as I have heard the Dalai Lama say on several occasions: "The great truths are all the same." I was seeing the sameness. I was living and breathing and practicing the sameness. And I was an American woman, a minister of a church that refers to what it teaches as practical Christianity.

A way to embrace the message of Jesus on a very practical level is to take these treasured teachings of Jesus and apply one or another to any of life's circumstances. We are not about worshipping Jesus Christ; rather we direct our spiritual paths toward becoming a Christed being just as Buddhists aspire to become a Buddha. Regardless of the label one places on it, the sea of our Divine nature lies in every one of us. The great joy with Tibetan Buddhism is the numerous phenomenal spiritual tools and formulas for living that lead to an awakened spiritual life.

These formulas offer tremendous value to the Western practitioner of spirituality, no matter what one's religious orientation. The formulas come to us from millennia ago overflowing with numbers: three of this; six of that; four of another having eight within it. As he read this book, my editor frequently pointed out that I was writing about yet another number. I did not make up these numbers, but I do believe I am one who can help you, the reader, navigate through them in such a way that you can understand and utilize them to better your life. You need not be overwhelmed.

My journey is extraordinary and blessed, and it is one I have always wanted to understand on deeper and deeper levels. Since that first trip in 1991, I have studied with the Dalai Lama numerous times. I have traveled to France to the monastery of Vietnam monk Thich Nhat Hanh, from whom I have incorporated so much wisdom and keen insight into my journey, which I share with you later in this book. This Zen monk, who left his home country during the Vietnam war to take part in peace negotiations in France, was forbidden by his government to return to his war-torn homeland.

What the Buddhists teach is a soul science. "Buddhism promotes understanding, not belief. Christianity promotes belief, not understanding," says noted American Buddhist scholar Dr. Robert Thurman. This simple statement sums up these two spiritual paths succinctly and clearly and points out their differences.

Tibetan Buddhism's teachings are so valuable because over the course of 2,500 years the monks and nuns have consistently practiced and refined them, sharing knowledge of how the soul works. In Buddhism it is said there are literally 84,000 teachings. I will offer the key teachings of Buddhism in this book, which is a result of my personal journey.

Buddhism, I believe, can work in concert with Christianity to create an ever-growing spiritual synergy. It has done and continues to do that for me. It has always been and continues to be of utmost importance to me that whatever I study or practice or teach be psychologically sound. This was a key factor in my coming into Unity and remains so to this day. It is my personal lens through which I evaluate a teaching or philosophy.

For one just beginning an exploration of Buddhism, it can be a daunting undertaking. What I've done in this book is taken the major concepts that I've studied for seventeen years and set out to explain them for the Western reader.

The Lotus Still Blooms deeply explores a number of the major tenets of Buddhism in a methodical and practical manner that can immediately be practiced by the reader.

Taking my cue from where the Buddha began, I have begun with the Four Noble Truths and followed them with the Eight-fold Path. The subsequent chapters are all based upon teachings I have gleaned primarily from His Holiness the Dalai Lama, but also from other Buddhist monks and nuns.

This material has liberated and transformed my life and the lives of many whom I have taught. It can do the same for you if you read and study and practice. May the message of *The Lotus Still Blooms* fill your heart daily with inspiration and the deep desire for your own life to be liberated.

The lotus symbolizes the gorgeous flower that rises out of the mud of this world. It is a symbol of purity and spontaneous Divine birth. It is said to be the throne of the Buddha. May it come to be your throne of wisdom and love, as the lotus still blooms in you.

We all have spiritual gifts, and I have long been told that one of my greatest is to take complex concepts on spiritual subjects and teach and explain them in a practical and understandable manner that can be utilized in one's day-to-day living. May this be the case for you. While you read and study this book, I hold this prayer for you:

May you be filled with loving kindness.
May you be well.
May you be peaceful and at ease.
May you be happy.

Joan Gattuso
Molokai, Hawaii

We see the Buddha as physician to the world . . .
In the Four Noble Truths he gives his clinical observations
on the human condition, then his diagnosis,
then the prognosis, and finally the cure.

—EKNATH ESWARAN

THE FOUR NOBLE TRUTHS

THERE ARE SO MANY "secrets" being revealed today. There is the landmark work *The Secret*. Although interesting and inspiring, it certainly does not contain any hitherto unknown esoteric secrets. Napoleon Hill's classic *Think and Grow Rich* offers numerous secrets that, if you discover them, will lead you to wealth and fulfillment. In recent history there have been any number of books that offer the secret to success, the secret to happiness, the secret to perfect weight, the secret to raising brilliant children, the secret to brilliant career moves, the secret to attracting a loving partner.

What is it with all these "secrets"? Are they really secrets at all, or is the secret simply to throw out the bait and see how many looking for a quick fix will grab the minnow? My colleagues and I chuckle and wonder why something is called a "secret" when it is something we have known and taught for decades. A minister friend of mine says, "People can feel important and special if they believe they are being let in on a secret that others don't know." He's right, in my opinion, and certainly book publishers and authors (including me) will use whatever ploys and hooks are needed to sell books and sell lots of them.

In Buddhism there are treasures, often called "precious jewels," but they are not necessarily secrets. In my understanding all the hyperbole about secret teachings pales in the light of the magnitude of the eternal truths contained within the Four Noble Truths and the Eight-fold Path, which are followed by thousands of advanced teachings available to the true seeker.

In Tibetan Buddhism there are deep teachings given only to advanced practitioners, usually monks and nuns, after years and years of study. The master teacher decides if the student is ready, and only then is this deep, complicated material taught. That is not what *The Lotus Still Blooms* is attempting.

Although the teachings on these pages are not swaddled in hype and the promise of a quick fix and easy riches, they do, as the Buddha taught, point the way to awakening and enlightenment. They outline a path to embrace and walk that begins to answer life's profound questions, not just for a moment but for all time. Hopefully these lessons will inspire you as you begin to practice and learn these eternal truths. Hopefully they will give you tools and formulas that are applicable to absolutely every aspect of life. **They are not secrets but truths.** They are without equal. They are fabulous and thrilling. They are the Four Noble Truths. They are noble because they are without equal. They are truths because these four are perhaps the greatest summation of the mystery enfolding human existence. They contain the diagnosis, the prognosis and the cure for the human condition.

Here is the answer that was first taught 2,600 years ago by the Buddha. It still excites me to the extent that my heart rejoices. I am enlivened to share these truths with you. They are clearly and succinctly stated so that you may understand them and perhaps change your life.

So let us begin at the beginning.

This beginning of Prince Siddhartha's life-changing journey would

When the Buddha was still known as Prince Siddhartha, he journeyed for the first time outside the protection of the palace walls and saw what is called "the four sights of the Buddha." What he saw was:

1. An elderly man. The Prince had no knowledge of aging, be it a person, animal or flower, since he had been totally sheltered from all perceived negativity by his father, the King.
2. A sick man. He was stunned when he saw him and asked his companion Chonna, "What is wrong?" Chonna explained, "It is the law of nature that we are all prone to sickness. Poor, rich, ignorant or wise, we are all creatures with bodies and so susceptible to disease."
3. A dead man. The Prince had never witnessed death. Explained Chonna, "He who begins life must end it."
4. An encounter with a monk who had a begging bowl. Again Chonna, "He has understood that beauty will turn to ugliness, youth into old age, life into death. And he is looking for the eternal, looking for that which does not die."

turn his world upside down, as it has done for the millions who have followed the Buddha's teachings through the aeons. The Buddha vowed, as he sat in meditation under a bodhi tree, that he would not arise until he achieved enlightenment, the supreme state of absolute transcendence and clarity. And that is what occurred.

After achieving enlightenment, the Buddha rose from under the bodhi tree and in a serene spot delivered his first message to a small band of future followers. This has come to be known as the Deer Park Sermon, where the first turning of the wheel of the Dharma (the body of spiritual teaching) took place. This is where the Buddha first taught what would become the essential teachings of Buddhism, the Four Noble Truths.

Many have allowed the first Noble Truth, "Life is suffering," to frighten them and have been unwilling to look further. When properly understood and taken within the context of the entire four, it is not frightening, it is enlightening. Here are the four:

THE FOUR NOBLE TRUTHS
1. Life is suffering.
2. The cause of suffering is our own grasping and clinging, our attachments to our desires.
3. Cessation of suffering is possible.
4. Presentation of the Eight-fold Path that leads to the end of suffering and promotes well-being.

The wise and scholarly have noted that the 84,000 teachings found within Tibetan Buddhism can be summarized by the Four Noble Truths. It takes real willingness to look at the first Noble Truth in order to become aware of another way and to recognize that this spiritual truth is your reality. Life contains suffering. Many are experiencing suffering at this very moment. Pick up any newspaper, turn on the evening news, look deeply at the lives of those around you, look deeply into your own life. Suffering will be found at every turn, because suffering is an inescapable fact of life, because life and its pleasures and ills are impermanent.

In magical thinking we wish the good and pleasurable aspects of life would last forever, just like the noble prince's father, the King. Nothing on our bodies would ever sag or wrinkle, our children would always adore us, our parents would never grow old and die. Nor would we grow old and die.

The entire subject of impermanence is often ignored by metaphysicians, somehow caught up in the magical thinking that—if we do not look at the unsettling aspects of life such as disease, aging and death as the Buddha saw on his first journey beyond the palace walls—undesired events will not occur in our lives. This is not a psychologically sound way to approach life, yet many are caught in such upside-down thinking.

The Buddhist teaching is that our attempt to avoid *all* aspects of life is the cause of our suffering. By acknowledging the full spectrum of our human experiences, we take the crucial first step toward alleviating our suffering.

When we are willing to mature in our thinking, we can then begin to understand that life is always in a state of flux. Everything is always changing in the world. The only aspect of life that does not change is the absolute—call it God or Christ nature, your Buddha nature, the Holy Spirit. We must draw our strength and find refuge from and in the Divine. All else is impermanent.

I attended a ten-day retreat based on the teachings of Sogyal Rinpoche and his magnificent book *The Tibetan Book of Living and Dying*. The retreat was held at a lovely lodge in a bucolic setting in Northern California. I personally had gone through much effort and expense to get there, traveling more than six thousand miles in the middle of a long-awaited, three-month sabbatical.

On the first day of the retreat the approximately 350 retreatants learned that Sogyal Rinpoche had been hospitalized as soon as he arrived in the United States from Europe. His senior students would carry on in his stead. There was much disappointment, myself included, but surely he, a Rinpoche and recognized spiritual master, would be well quickly and released from the hospital to assume his role as leader and teacher.

But that did not happen. He was released after several days, but he was in need of rest and recuperation. He telephoned the retreatants and spoke very mindfully on impermanence and the nature of illness. He implied that even the great ones can get sick. He said, "Illness is a kind of warning, a reminder. We believe we have time, we believe we have time, we believe we have time—and then we have no time." He was living for us all in what he called "the ever-present theme of impermanence."

When we embrace the universality of impermanence, we are then no longer thrown off our pins when it stops to pay a call in our life or in the life of a loved one. Do you sometimes look in the mirror and see your mother's face looking back at you? That's impermanence. Can you barely get out of bed in the morning because of all your many aches and pains? That's impermanence. A child gets sick and dies. That's impermanence. A young soldier does not return from Iraq. That's impermanence. The most glorious vacation comes to an end. That's impermanence. You now live in an "empty nest" where your nuclear family once lived. That's impermanence. The examples are endless, and each one causes us to suffer to the degree that we are attached.

Take some quiet time and consider how impermanence has arisen for you personally and how you have met it. You might want to take a moment to reflect on five major events that have impacted your life. If it causes you to be fearful, release that in meditation over and over. Know that even in the midst of great change, you remain safe because of your eternal connection with God, with your Buddha self, with your Christ self. You and your Divine self are one, and that can never change. That is permanent, and how blessed you are when you realize that this is so.

THE FIRST NOBLE TRUTH

During that retreat Sogyal Rinpoche said that the First Noble Truth could be better understood by limiting your thinking to "life *is* suffering." It is not simply that life causes us to suffer, but rather "samsara" is suffering. Samsara is this delusional world we have been conditioned to see as real, but it is not real. It is the endless cycle of birth, life, death and rebirth over and over again. The Dalai Lama called samsara "unenlightened existence." And when we insist the world be what it is not, we cause ourselves to suffer. Why is life—samsara—suffering? It is because nothing in this world is permanent. When we recognize rather than deny the fact of impermanence and its tie to suffering, we have taken the first step.

THE SECOND NOBLE TRUTH

The Second Noble Truth is quite logical. We experience suffering because we cling, grasp, have unmet expectations, have addictions. A while back I saw a TV feature on women addicted to plastic surgery. These weren't the common eye lift, face-lift or tummy tuck. These women had dozens upon dozens of surgeries. One young woman still in the bloom of her youth at twenty-nine had had more surgeries than her age.

I am definitely one for taking the best care that we can of our physical selves. But no matter what we do, we are—as the years roll by—getting older, having a sickness or two or more, perhaps experiencing an accident or two. And each one of us is going to die, as well as everyone you love. Cling to this not happening and you will just suffer all the more.

THE THIRD NOBLE TRUTH

The good news begins with the Third Noble Truth, the cessation of suffering. There is a way out, since suffering is not our eternal fate. If we are willing to look deeply at the nature of life, we can rise up and truly experience happiness. On a number of occasions I have heard His Holiness the Dalai Lama say that the purpose of life is to be happy. The happy life begins when we realize that life is boundless. This can only come as the result of looking deeply at what is, rather than what we wish it to be.

THE FOURTH NOBLE TRUTH

Here is the really good news! The Fourth Noble Truth explains how we can achieve happiness through engaging fully in the Noble Eight-fold Path. Here we find the cure to our suffering. We can call it "spiritual medicine" or "soul medicine." We must ingest this medicine and take the teachings out of the textbooks and into our hearts and lives.

Remember, clinical observation of the Four Noble Truths can be summed up as the diagnosis, the prognosis, the cure, and engaging in the cure. Buddha did not teach the extinction of all desire (trishna). Our desire can become zeal, enthusiasm toward our spiritual awakening. Nothing is overcome (i.e., desire) by crushing it, only by transforming it. The Tibetan Buddhist scholar Dr. Robert Thurman said, "We can each become a noble person, and all of us are destined to do so."

I had a conversation on wanting good and pleasant experiences in my life with my Hawaiian cardiologist, Dr. Hinson Chun, a Tibetan Buddhist. He said, "Of course we must have pure 'desire' to ever make progress on the Eight-fold Path." When we engage in the cure, we move into the Eight-fold Path. It is how we can systematically cease doing what causes us to suffer and embrace the eight steps that lead to a noble life and happiness.

All that I am is the result of all that I have thought.

—BUDDHA

What we are today comes from our thoughts of yesterday,
and our present thoughts build our life of tomorrow:
our life is the creation of our mind.
If a man acts or speaks with an impure mind,
suffering follows him as the wheel of the cart follows
the beast that draws the cart.
What we are today comes from our thoughts of yesterday,
and our present thoughts build our life of tomorrow:
our life is the creation of our mind.
If a man speaks or acts with a pure mind,
joy follows him as his own shadow.

—THE DHAMMAPADA, VERSES 1–2

INTRODUCTION TO THE EIGHT-FOLD PATH

THE EIGHT-FOLD PATH, the Fullness of the Fourth Noble Truth, offers a timeless blueprint for living the spiritually realized life. It was first offered by the Buddha at his very first sermon, called the "Deer Park Sermon," delivered at Benares, India.

Here for the first time the Four Noble Truths were presented, followed

As the Buddha introduced his first teaching on the Middle Path, he instructed the monks as follows:

1. Now this, monks, is the noble truth of pain: birth is painful, old age is painful, sickness is painful, death is painful, sorrow, lamentation, dejection and despair are painful. Contact with unpleasant things is painful, not getting what one wishes is painful. In short the five groups of grasping are painful.
2. Now this, monks, is the noble truth of the cause of pain: the craving which tends to rebirth, combined with pleasure and lust, finding pleasure here and there; namely the craving for passion, the craving for existence, the craving for nonexistence.
3. Now this, monks, is the noble truth of the cessation of pain, the cessation without a remainder of craving, the abandonment, forsaking release, nonattachment.
4. Now this, monks, is the noble truth of the way that leads to the cessation of pain: this is the noble Eight-fold Way; namely Right View, Right Thought, Right Speech, Right Action, Right Livelihood, Right Effort, Right Mindfulness, Right Concentration.

by the Eight-fold Path, which are really the steps of the Fourth Noble Truth. Again they are: Right View, Right Thought, Right Speech, Right Action, Right Livelihood, Right Effort, Right Mindfulness, Right Concentration.

A chapter has been created for each, illustrating how each has been applied in my life and how I have in turn taught its value and use to others. Each of the eight chapters offers practical, real-life examples, along with exercises to assist the reader in integrating each step into his or her own life.

The first two steps, Right View and Right Thought, give the reader the preliminary conditions that must be established in the individual's life in order to make further spiritual progress. The third, fourth and fifth—Right Speech, Right Action, Right Livelihood—speak of one's willingness to align these most important aspects of life with one's spiritual intentions. Here the practitioner learns to live his life consistent with this high aspiration. Also, the foundation is laid to progress to the final three—Right Effort, Right Mindfulness, Right Concentration.

These final three are the fundamental conditions necessary to progress toward ultimately achieving an awakened mind or enlightenment.

The Eight-fold Path is a methodical process for moving toward an enlightened state of being using spiritual tools to get there. Tibetan Buddhism has preserved the enormous treasury of what is original Indian Buddhism, the studies of the ultimate nature of being. To attain Buddhahood/Christhood requires a radical shift in consciousness. Buddhism teaches that the old paradigm has to go. Suffering, victimhood and separation become union, empowerment and oneness when one spends years, if not lifetimes, studying and practicing Buddhist principles. The Eight-fold Path is key to this growth.

If an individual has a calm state of mind, that person's
attitudes and views will be calm and tranquil,
even in the presence of great agitation.

—HIS HOLINESS THE DALAI LAMA

RIGHT VIEW

RIGHT VIEW IS THE first point on the Buddhist Eight-fold Path. Here is where one begins the journey of living as a Noble Being. What exactly is a Noble Being? It is one who cares for others as much as she cares for herself. This requires a huge shift in consciousness, an enormous shift in perception. You are saying: "Others are as important as I am."

In this section a road map is presented, giving you tools to a path that, when followed, offers you an awakened state of consciousness. We can study, practice and come to know these eight points on a soul level. It is not sufficient just to know them intellectually. We must integrate their wisdom into our very essence. We must have our inner beliefs so joined with these ancient truths that we even *dream* them. Then we can begin to move into a more awakened consciousness and live our lives in a more conscious state.

In metaphysics this first point would be called spiritual understanding. By incorporating it into our lives, we begin to view life accurately—not simply according to our perceptions (clouded, mixed, muddled) but what is spiritually true in any given situation.

When we evaluate life through our perceptions we keep ourselves in a perpetual state of confusion. Perception keeps our lives in chaos. Our perceptions are legion. We have numerous perceptions about any given subject, and for the most part they are all terribly inaccurate!

The reason they are inaccurate is because we have been asleep. With Right View we no longer perceive life from an upside-down perspective, and our perceptions begin to right themselves. Then we can begin to "view" life accurately, truly, eternally. This takes tremendous spiritual commitment.

The Zen Buddhist Monk Thich Nhat Hanh speaks frequently in both his teaching and his writing of "watering seeds." The seeds you may be watering are seeds of being misunderstood, victimhood, judgment and deception, seeds of past hurts and sorrows. If you are, then you need to be watering seeds of kindness, loving action, forgiveness, love and compassion. These latter seeds are the seeds of Right View.

If we are watering seeds of "he done me wrong," we are watering seeds of misperception. The Buddha said on this subject, "Perception leads to deception." What a phenomenal yet simple way to convey this entire teaching. I've learned to repeat this statement frequently. It is most helpful.

We need to see others' suffering as our own.

—HIS HOLINESS THE DALAI LAMA

Right View is sometimes called Right Understanding. Our Right View begins with a deep understanding. Says Thich Nhat Hanh, "When we can come to truly understand impermanence . . . then it could be said we have Right View."

With Right View we can begin to recognize those beliefs, views and concepts that have caused us to suffer, and we can begin to learn how *not* to water them and increase their strength.

In Right View we water the seeds of truth—loving-kindness, generosity, goodness, compassion, loyalty, selflessness—and these views blossom and grow within us. We learn to water and nurture the beneficial and wholesome seeds in us, those that are part of our Buddha nature, and we cease watering the angry, mistrustful, selfish, fearful seeds. Over time we will see huge shifts in our perceptions and advancement on our spiritual path.

Our perceptions are attached to illusions rather than the truth. That gets us into soul trouble. We live as if a false belief is totally true, and this causes us to suffer and suffer greatly. What needs to occur and occur constantly is intense self-examination. To be vigilant is to be introspective. This takes a highly disciplined mind and an enormous willingness to live a different life. But doing so results in a life that is becoming more and more free of suffering. Sogyal Rinpoche teaches that, when one is angry, 90 percent of one's perception is distorted. So it is essential to resolve one's anger in order to have Right View.

Other ways for a Westerner to grasp Right View is to recall the words of Paul from the New Testament: "I look in a mirror darkly." We cannot see because of the clouding of the mirror of our minds. Another common expression is: "Do you see the glass half full or half empty?" In other words, what seeds are we watering?

The current means for most of us seeing our "view" is the result of our accumulated memories, teachings and experiences, all stored in our subconscious minds. It is easy to believe our perceptions are accurate. They are not. We have the wrong view and don't even realize it.

The Buddhists call that which fills the subconscious mind "store consciousness." Each person's store consciousness is uniquely his. That is why a dozen people can each have a different perception of any given situation or event.

Please, my young brothers and sisters, please take more attention on your inner values. That's very important.

—HIS HOLINESS THE DALAI LAMA

I believe an accurate understanding of Right View is very important for Westerners. We have been so conditioned to believe that our happiness comes from the outer, such as the accumulation of more possessions. If we have more and more, bigger and better, then we will be happy. Or perhaps we believe that more educational degrees will make us happy. Or perhaps we think it's knowing the right people, belonging to the right club, going to the right parties, receiving recognition and awards. Many Americans view success as living through their children's accomplishments, even living their lives *for* their children. These are all wrong view, because someday all of the preceding are going to cause you to suffer. Someday you will see they are all impermanent with no enduring reality.

The door will close in your face. You'll be passed over for the award. Your child will resent you. Someone will come along who is more educated, more clever, more handsome and on and on. You will suffer because you mistakenly believed your happiness was circumstance-dependent rather than knowing that the impermanent can never bring about happiness.

An affirmation you can use to change this "outer" thinking is: "My happiness comes only from that which is eternal." From time to time I meditate on that affirmation, and it brings much clarity to my mind, helping me to really know what is truly valuable. And I have discovered these valuable truths for myself: love, caring, kindness, sharing, generosity, a peaceful mind, peaceful perceptions, compassion, understanding. These are the seeds in my life that I water daily.

Right View is truly seeing life as it is, not as it appears to be in the outer. As I write this, it is just a few days past the London suicide bombings of three underground stations and one double-decker bus. In the West our collective head is spinning over the shock of it all. We question how this could happen and happen in of all places the seat of civility, London. The four young men, three born in England and all raised there, by all appearances were totally integrated into British culture. Yet their secretly held views were anything but pro-British. While they plotted their destructive plan, those who lived with them and knew them had no clue of their sinister scheme. Most would agree they harbored wrong view.

Anytime anyone believes some benefit can come forth by causing another to suffer, it is the opposite of Right View. It is wrong view. Unwholesome seeds of hate were watered by these young men. We must be very mindful to water only wholesome seeds so they are what blooms in us and in our children.

Thich Nhat Hanh sums up Right View with this teaching: "From the viewpoint of ultimate reality, Right View is the absence of all views." Right View is realizing that the true nature of the mind is the true nature of everything. This is the absolute truth.

Our perceptions deceive us, pure and simple. They cannot be trusted. Perceptions lead to deceptions. And when we begin to realize this, we begin to wake up. In order to experience Right View we have to make the connection between what is manifesting in our lives and what seeds we are watering.

Right View is distinct from Right Thought, but all are linked. Right View is a challenging concept, an ultimate concept. With the very highest expression of Right View we relinquish our judgments, good or ill, about everything. Who has accomplished this? Not many. But when we grasp it, we can end our suffering.

When the historical Buddha first began to teach, he knew in his awakened mind that it was possible to end suffering and to cease being miserable. It *is* possible to end being miserable, but we must start with an accurate view of an experience. These are the seeds we must water.

*. . . Everything depends on mind. Our life is shaped by our
mind; we become what we think. Suffering follows an evil
thought as the wheel of the cart follows the oxen that draw it.
Joy follows a pure thought like a shadow that never leaves.*

—THE DHAMMAPADA

RIGHT THOUGHT

THINKING IS THE SPEECH of the mind. This is such a simple and
profound way to define our own thinking. When our thinking is
aligned with Right View, we are thinking clearly in accord with the highest ideals. *A Course in Miracles* speaks of upside-down thinking, and the
Buddhists have a term for this, "viparyasa," which translates as "upside-
down way."

Often we are caught in upside-down thinking. Our greatest challenge
is that we don't recognize it as being upside down. We think we are right.
We think our perceptions and thoughts are accurate. They are not. Me-
dieval man thought the world was flat, but it did not make it flat. We
could say they had wrong view and wrong thought.

Here are some suggestions for ways to prevent upside-down thinking,
or wrong thought:

1. Associate with like-minded friends and acquaintances. When
   this is not possible, say because of a negative work environment, know there is always something you can do. My friend

Shirley, a teacher, would find herself becoming greatly troubled by the critical, judgmental, victim-like conversation in the teachers' lunchroom. Years ago she took control and began to have lunch alone in her classroom. Daily she would begin her lunch period with a fifteen- to twenty-minute meditation. Then silently and mindfully she would enjoy her lunch, followed by ten to fifteen minutes of inspirational reading. After her mindful lunch, she felt refreshed and renewed and ready for her afternoon students.

2. Faithfully keep a daily spiritual practice, centering yourself in true thoughts frequently throughout the day. Do this by keeping spiritual reading material handy and referring to it often. Take a soul break by entering into your inner spirit for three to five minutes.

3. Keep an affirmation or mantra handy to repeat, especially when you are being pulled into a judgmental or fearful situation. Use mala beads and repeat a set of ten two or three times a day using your mantra.

These practices are supportive in keeping you on track daily. Think of it as a spiritual diet. Feeding your soul is equally as important as feeding your body.

Ralph Waldo Emerson said, "We become what we think about all day long." Be ever mindful of what your thoughts beneath your thoughts might be. Think in accord with that which is spiritually true, good, kind, helpful, loving.

In order to have Right Thinking we must have it in the foundation of Right View. Our minds must be constantly trained and every thought mindfully witnessed in order to move into Right View.

All that I am is the result of all that I have thought.

—THE DHAMMAPADA

Our thinking is constantly creating our reality. The easiest way to observe your past thinking is to look at what is present in your life today. Whatever it may be is a certain indicator of where your thinking has been.

Buddhism has a special gift for helping people
calm their minds.

—HIS HOLINESS THE DALAI LAMA

In Buddhism there are three practices that instruct us in Right Thought that are very helpful in creating a calm mind:

First: There is a practice to frequently ask yourself, "Are you sure?" Are you sure your thinking about a person or a situation is accurate? Or is it just a story you are telling yourself? This humorous story illustrates the point.

After several years of observing him do it, a woman in my congregation asked me why it was my husband, David, left the 9 A.M. service immediately preceding the offering. For years she had thought he left at that moment as some sort of cosmic act not to be in the sanctuary when the tithes and offerings were being given and received. Her thinking told her something to the effect that he did not feel it was appropriate for the minister's husband to be in the room during that part of the service. In actuality he always left the service at that point to go to another part of the building to be on time to facilitate a *Course in Miracles* study group. Her perception was essentially a story she had made up.

When she revealed to me what her self-talk story had convinced her was true, I burst out laughing. I dropped my usually unflappable platform, ministerial persona and laughed heartily. It was slightly embarrassing. She had been attending only the 9 A.M. service for years. If she had attended the 11 A.M. service, she would have observed David staying through the offering and even giving his weekly tithe.

Are you sure about what you are sure about?

To help bring clarity to your mind by asking, "Are you sure?" I suggest creating several flash cards containing only those words written in bold script in your own handwriting. Place them where they will be most frequently seen: in your journal, taped to mirrors in your home, on the dashboard of your car, at your desk, at your computer. Place at least four or five around your environment.

Our thinking can be far off the mark, and we can be so out of touch. We can use Right View by asking, "Are you sure?" This is a place to begin to right our thinking.

Second: Ask, "What am I doing?" or, as Dr. Phil of TV fame so perfectly asks in response to people's outlandish behavior, "What were you thinking?" When you create needless stress, ask: "What am I doing?" When you are anxious, ask: "What am I doing?" When you feel anger rising, ask: "What am I doing?" When you speak unkindly of another, ask: "What am I doing?" When you harbor ill feelings or resentments, ask: "What am I doing?" When you water seeds of negativity, ask: "What am I doing?" When you are racing through your life or through a simple task, ask: "What am I doing?" When your cosmic plate has become a platter and is overflowing, ask, "What am I doing?"

In the 1960s Ram Dass popularized the phrase "Be here now." These concepts lead to self-awakening and bring us fully into the present moment, which is the only place we can know the truth. When we are swept up in the trauma of life, living with unskilled rather than skilled behavior, it is good to stop and ask ourselves, "What am I doing?" When anger rises in us, let us ask, "What am I doing?" Whenever we feel victimized, ask, "What am I doing?"

We are such habitual creatures, we repeat a habit, energy, an attitude, a behavior without much forethought. We need to be aware when we are doing this, and one way to do this is to say to ourselves, "Hello, habit energy." We can then begin to notice our habitual, compulsive, ceaseless thoughts. Sometimes it is simply a habit to worry or to be distracted. If at these moments we can pause, recognize the habitual behaviors and greet them, we can begin to learn to get past them.

Third: Ask, "Is this helpful?" This is a phrase I resonated toward when I first heard it. It is like a reality barometer. Is this gossiping conversation helpful? Is this attitude helpful? Is this prejudice helpful? Is this fear helpful? Is this anger helpful? Is this guilt helpful? Is this long-held belief helpful? Is holding family secrets helpful?

We all can carry hidden beliefs—attitudes based on fear and negative programming from our family, culture and society that keep us separated from one another. These beliefs keep us asleep.

Is this helpful? This simple, clear question is a way to assist us living mindfully. In the moment-by-moment living of our lives, this question is a simple way to explore our thoughts, beliefs and attitudes. This leads to our healing, to our becoming a more whole, aware human being, to becoming a person living out of an attitude of loving kindness, rather than living from hate, fear and prejudice.

A word I fell in love with in my earliest years of studying Buddhism was "bodhichitta." Bodhichitta is the manifestation of compassion, grace, love and goodness, all rolled up together. When we welcome and strive to express bodhichitta energy, we long to assist all others in realizing freedom from suffering. Bodhichitta translates as "the enlightened essence of the heart," or "the heart of our enlightened mind." The great Buddhist saint Shantideva called bodhichitta "the supreme elixir, the inexhaustible treasure, the supreme medicine, the tree that shelters all beings."

Studying Right Thought has helped me go deeper into the difficult lesson in life that deals with our thoughts and the concept that in the early stages of our journey we are seldom aware of our true thoughts. Our true thoughts are buried deep within our minds underneath the monkey-mind chatter, the habitual and the unconscious thinking. In order to reach these true, inner thoughts we must learn to still the mind through faithful meditation practices.

The Buddha said that the broader the student's consciousness, the more profound is his experience of the teaching. Intellectual learning must be applied to one's own life, into one's own practice.

Knowledge, practice and a compassionate heart must all be united in a true teacher. It is taught that there are ten qualities all true teachers embody. They are: (1) Disciplined mind. (2) Calm mind. (3) Calm being. (4) Knowledge that exceeds students'. (5) Enthusiasm for teaching. (6) Vast learning. (7) Realization of emptiness, a commitment to practice compassion. (8) Eloquent and skillful teaching. (9) Deep compassion toward students. (10) Resilience and ultimate patience with students.

The student's qualities need to be (1) An open mind. (2) An objective mind. (3) The intelligence to discern what is accurate from what is inaccurate. (4) Enthusiasm.

The essence of spiritual practice is to be a better person and to refrain from harming others.

I think when tragic things happen, it is on the surface.
It is like the ocean. On the surface a wave comes,
and sometimes the wave is very serious and strong.
But it comes and goes, comes and goes, and underneath
the ocean always remains calm.

—HIS HOLINESS THE DALAI LAMA

And we must learn to always remain calm at our depths, like the ocean at its depths.

The Buddhists say all things and events lack self-existence. The teaching states that all things are impermanent and are an illusion. One of the greatest insights I have ever taken away from the Dalai Lama was when he said, "We can say something is an illusion, not because my writing tablet, desk and pen are not here, but we can certainly say and agree that they are impermanent." Therefore, anything that is impermanent can be said to be an illusion because it is impermanent. It will not last forever.

The next logical conclusion is that the mind eventually reaches this level of awareness. The ultimate nature of reality is the emptiness of all things and events—the absence of independent reality. Nothing can cease the continuation of consciousness or mind. Emptiness is not nothingness. It means it does not have its own origination. This is the Middle Way. This can be most challenging for our Western minds to comprehend.

The mind can be likened to the ocean viewed from an airplane at 35,000 feet. It looks completely calm, yet when you near the surface, you find much turbulence if a storm is in progress. So, too, our minds appear to be calm and serene, but when we look inside, there can be much monkey-mind chatter and much turmoil and raging turbulence.

Our lifelong task is to learn to still the mind—to free the mind of angry thoughts, sad thoughts, depressed thoughts, separate thoughts, lonely thoughts, hateful thoughts, thoughts of attachment. The only means of doing this is constant practice and observation, replacing an angry thought with a calm thought, a sad thought with a joyous thought. We must practice deep meditation.

After much practice, the troubled mind can be put to rest, and then the basic nature of the mind can rise. Our basic nature is serene, clear, calm.

In order to have Right Thought, Thich Nhat Hanh says that we must embody the Four Immeasurables—Love, Compassion, Joy and Equanimity. They are the very nature of a noble being, an enlightened being. We must stop feeding our negative states of mind. How? We cease from calling violence "entertainment." We cease speaking endlessly of ourselves as the victim. We begin to see it as our lesson, our karma. We cease from watering those seeds, and we learn our lessons and go on.

We must be willing to look head-on at our suffering and what causes us to suffer. If we try to avoid this meeting, our suffering will continue to be the engine that runs our lives, filling our experience with more and more suffering. When we focus on suffering, sure as day follows night, more suffering will present itself.

Personally, in dealing with mentally tormenting situations, ones that seem to grab us by the throat and not let go, I have found it takes tremendous energy, focus and unwavering commitment to move out of consuming negative thoughts and to shift back into the true nature of my mind.

Lama Chonam, dear friend and Buddhist teacher, once said while teaching at my church, "Sometimes our individual and collective mind has to be shocked into seeing the nature of reality." He said this in direct response to 9/11, when those two jets roared into the Twin Towers in New York City, a third slammed deep into the earth of rural Pennsylvania and a fourth smashed into the Pentagon. As Americans, our collective mind was shocked to its core. The unimaginable and unspeakable had occurred. We saw the images either up close or on television, and initially few of us could grasp what was happening.

I recall that I was working at home and had stopped and turned on the television just as the first jet struck. My mind could not comprehend what my eyes had just seen. I instantly began praying and doing my utmost to remain centered. In those moments we still did not know that the horror was intentional. As that gruesome reality began to be revealed when the second jet hit the second tower, I knew I had to drive the thirty minutes to my church to be with my staff. As I drove through several suburbs of Cleveland, it was surreal. There were so few cars on the roads. At stoplights fellow drivers would look back as I looked over, and in stunned silence we would nod. It was like driving through a dream in slow motion.

For America this was one of the worst possible illustrations of wrong thought. At times it seemed as if the world had gone stark raving mad. Congregants of mine were vacationing in Hawaii at a serene, exclusive resort when the news of the attacks on the Twin Towers began to spread.

They were having breakfast on the lanai when guests began intently watching a television set reporting the tragedy. A Muslim woman standing next to my congregants' table began to jump up and down with glee,

THE LOTUS STILL BLOOMS · 33

clapping her hands. Apparently she could not even remotely contain her happiness at the suffering of our country, where, at that moment, she was a guest.

My congregants were so terrified not only by what was occurring but also by the hatred playing out before them that they immediately went back to their room, packed up and took the next flight to Honolulu. They did not want to be on a remote island, not knowing what was going to be happening next, and they felt very frightened of that woman and her hate-filled reaction.

Buddhist teachers would instruct that we must have compassion for ones exhibiting such upside-down thinking and behavior. I can understand that, as could my congregants, that they chose not to be at the same resort as that Muslim woman—a choice many of us might make under the circumstances.

Right Thinking is always in alignment with the spiritual ideal.

Better than a speech of a thousand vain words is one
thoughtful word which brings peace to the mind.

—*THE DHAMMAPADA*, VERSE 100

RIGHT SPEECH

THE SPIRITUAL DISCIPLINES I have learned during many years study-ing Tibetan Buddhism have become so much a part of me that I have begun to constantly have insights and realizations on the ultimate nature of reality. There is a point where *all* teachings converge and the common thread of truth can be seen. It is happening in my life, and I am endeavor-ing to share how it can occur with you.

Right Speech is the third aspect on the eight-spoked wheel of the Eight-fold Path. The expression and understanding of Right Speech is absolutely crucial on our spiritual journey if we are to attain an enlight-ened life.

When we practice Right Speech, we are constantly mindful of the vibra-tion and impact upon ourselves and others of all the words we speak. If all of us were truly mindful of all our words, how different they would be.

With every utterance, a vibration is sent forth. Therefore, when we speak angry words, harsh words, toxic words, curse words, a like vibration is emanating from us and enfolding us and those around us like a blanket. On the other hand, when we speak words of loving-kindness, compas-sion, caring, tenderness, a vibration in kind is being sent out and embrac-ing all. These vibrations, negative or positive, do not dissipate quickly.

Thich Nhat Hanh, the Vietnamese Buddhist Monk with whom I have studied in France, has said that we in our Western culture are very quick to turn to anger. I could not agree more. We so quickly become irritated over insignificant things, small matters, that we soon escalate to a state of uncontrollable anger. Our speech reflects our misperceptions as we attempt to make things matter that do not.

To live as conscious beings we must practice Right Speech every moment of our lives—not just our waking moments. We must bring this awareness even into our dreams, so that even in our dream states we become more aware. As we become more conscious and learn to do so, the living of our lives begins to become seamless. And this awareness in time will even filter down into our dreams. What we perceive in our awake reality begins to wed to our dream states. These different realities of mind begin to become connected, and a universal consistency begins to emerge.

In Right Speech we realize that absolutely every utterance has an impact on us, on those around us, on our animals, on our plants, on our environment. Therefore, we cease from saying anything that would harm, such as swearing and using words in anger that become toxic. This takes tremendous effort and a retraining of our minds It does not mean we suppress, but it does mean we learn to release the anger and fear that results in harsh, unkind, sarcastic, caustic communication.

While driving with a friend, a delightful spiritual teacher, a driver on the freeway did an unconscious maneuver and caused the man with whom I was traveling to take quick action to avoid a collision, which he executed with skill. Then he started to swear a blue streak. It was every bit as rattling as the other driver's erratic moves. It wasn't the time to say anything to my friend, but it was a reminder that living consciously does not take a holiday when another person drives poorly. It takes constant practice, practice, practice to bring a life-transforming philosophy into *every* moment of our lives, even while driving on the freeway.

We do this first by being the observer and noticing what we are allowing to escape from our mouths. We hopefully are mature enough not to use the childish excuse, "I just can't help myself when those words come out of my mouth." The only person ever responsible is the person yelling and verbalizing anger.

Next we take the angry and fearful feelings we are about to express as harsh words and we consciously release them to: the clear light, a divine presence, a bodhisattva, etc. Next we are consciously aware *not* to go back and pick them up again. If our speech causes anyone to suffer, then it is not Right Speech.

The Buddha teaches that if we need to have a conversation with someone who is agitated, or who has a difficult personality, we need to continuously be mindful, consciously breathe in and breathe out, and listen deeply to that person for one hour. If, during that hour, you begin to feel agitated yourself, say to the other dear one, "I truly want to listen to you, but I find myself unable to continue. So let us agree to stop for now. Then in a few days, after much meditation, we can meet again." How often do we communicate with such an enlightened mind? Can you even imagine how blessed our world would be if we all began to communicate in such a way?

Right Speech is as much about how to speak and address others as it is about what to avoid. In Right Speech we learn to verbally encourage others. Once, a fellow minister reflecting on the giving nature of a well-known teacher, said: "She is the best cheerleader I have ever met. She always has an encouraging word and is quick to praise another's noble efforts and good works." What a lovely comment to make about someone—one who not only looks for and sees the good but takes the next step and praises it, as well.

In our Western society we have a harsh manner of communicating to friends and strangers alike. It tends to be both direct and impolite. How often do you say, "Excuse me," "Please," "Thank you so very much," "How kind," "How thoughtful of you" or even "Good-bye"?

Right Speech is called the sentinel at the door of our consciousness. Practicing Right Speech results in what the Buddhists call an accumulation of merits. In Christian thought and teachings we do not have a direct correlation, but we could make a broad comparison through the idea of attracting grace or gathering good karma into your life.

People will just naturally be more attracted to us the more we draw to ourselves good energy merits. We become a blessing to others and ourselves, as well. We cease from ever harming others through our words. As adults we live by the simple teachings most of us have been taught as children. Before speaking, check out the inner pulse of your communication.

* Is it kind?
* Is it helpful?
* Is it true?

It couldn't be easier or more direct. One would think it would not be so difficult to always and only speak words that are kind, helpful and true. We truly become the better person, deepening our spiritual path, expanding toward enlightenment.

A Hindu teacher gives this advice to his students about telling the truth: "Anyone who succeeds in telling the truth for twelve consecutive years will become enlightened." That is certainly a noble goal to aspire to—no fibbing, no half-truths, no white lies, only full, totally honest disclosure.

THE VALUE OF RIGHT SPEECH:
1. We draw merits to ourselves.
2. We are a blessing to all others.
3. We cease from harming others.
4. We cease from harming ourselves.
5. We become a better person.
6. We deepen our spiritual path.
7. We expand toward enlightenment.
8. We begin to understand the ultimate nature of reality.

In the early nineties I attended the Tucson, Arizona, teaching on Patience given by the Dalai Lama. It was modestly attended. Once, after the students formed an arc through which the Dalai Lama was to pass, we were instructed not to touch him or speak to him and to stay in a semi-bowed position, a sign of respect. There was great excitement in the air, and as he approached I felt so very blessed to be in such close proximity to this holy man. He was passing inches in front of me, as I held my hands in a prayerful pose and bowed.

The instant he was even with me, he abruptly stopped, snapped his head to the side and looked directly into my eyes. It took my breath away. All I can say is that it was an instant between us that was a holy encounter. It has remained with me to this moment. The Dalai Lama looked into me, and I was blessed. There have been a number of close encounters since, and of course they are all filled with goodness. But nothing could touch that first holy encounter. It left me speechless. And I have seldom spoken of it because it was so sacred for me. There are times when practicing Right Speech that it is appropriate to remain silent.

In Right Speech we are aware that our words can heal or harm. They can lift up or tear down. When we are in our right mind, why would we ever allow ourselves to harm or tear down another person through our words?

When we live in ignorance and not mindfully, we can allow our speech to come rushing out of us, and at times it seems it has bypassed our thought and has a life of its own. Andrew Harvey says, "Speech is the primary medium of enlightenment." The purpose of enlightenment is to serve all others. Right Speech is an outgrowth of Right Thinking. They cannot be separated.

One of the most effective methods to train the mind toward Right Speech is through the use of affirmations. Insert your own name in the affirmations following to personalize them. Here are some examples to get you started, but feel free to create your own. Just make sure they are focused on the positive and what you want, rather than what you don't want.

- I _____ am becoming more and more mindful of the words I speak.
- I _____ speak kind, loving, supportive words to family and friends.
- I _____ speak kind, loving, supportive words to all others, including myself.
- As I _____ practice Right Speech, I am becoming more aware in all areas of my life.
- I _____ am now using Right Speech in all my communications.
- Right Speech brings peace to my heart and mind.

The Dalai Lama suggests that before arising in our morning meditation we commit to being mindful of our speech throughout the day. At midday we check ourselves by asking, "How am I doing so far? Have my communications been clear, truthful and kind? Are there alterations to be made? Let me now adjust and go on with a fresh start." At the close of the day ask, "How did I do today?" Hopefully we can say we did really well and, if not, resolve to pay much closer attention to our speech tomorrow.

Dharma teaching is a mirror to look deeply, see what is being reflected and correct what is in error in body, speech and mind.

—HIS HOLINESS THE DALAI LAMA

Only the pursuit of spiritual richness over physical comfort
would lead humans to a peaceful world.

—HIS HOLINESS THE DALAI LAMA

RIGHT ACTION

❧

MOST SIMPLY STATED, Right Action means "do no harm." Always come from the space of the heart, be kind, live mindfully, practice conscious consumption.

Right Action is being certain that our every action is in accord with our inner essence. It is consistency of being—as within, so without. It is knowing when to act and when to be still, when to work in the outer realms and when to work in the inner realms.

When we do not practice Right Action, we cause ourselves so much suffering, and we cause great suffering to those around us, as well. When one is not consciously engaged in practicing Right Action, there is a disconnect between what is being thought, said and done. It is so easy today to witness this disconnection coming out of the behaviors of so many, whether they be celebrities or a professional colleague or your next-door neighbor. The following story illustrates this point:

Stephen thought he could "get away" with cruel, ruthless, cheating behaviors toward his devoted wife, Shelly, in order to continue to get what he wanted. But, as I had to keep telling my girlfriend Shelly, "He cannot." Friends of ours, they had been married for many years. They shared many interests, had similar backgrounds and education. He was a doctor, she a

Ph.D. It was a second marriage for both. The first years they appeared connected and happy, and although their lives were frequently focused on appearances, they were the typical affluent American couple, always accumulating more and better stuff, always upgrading.

Then an opportunity came to Stephen to have a surgical practice three to four days a week hundreds of miles from home. He took it and rented an apartment near the hospital, commuting home on weekends. Finally they moved from their primary home out of California, a community property state, to his new location, not a community property state, quite a distance from their former community and network of friends.

Alone every week, Shelly felt very isolated, lonely and disconnected away from her work and supportive women friends. She picked up a consulting job and was working sixty to seventy hours a week to fill her empty time and life. She would frequently call me for support and advice. I would urge her to seek a spiritual connection and community for support where she now lived. She was drawn to Buddhism and no longer found solace in the religion of her childhood. She read a few of the Buddhist books I recommended, but that was as far as her spiritual path went. She did not find a sangha, a spiritual community or anyone nearby to connect with on a soul level.

Stephen began spending more and more days away, and the gulf between them continued to widen. Red flags were flapping in the breeze of Shelly's life. I could see it. Her other friends could see it. Her siblings could see it. But as is so often the case in such circumstances, Shelly could not.

Then late one night the phone rang. Fearing something was wrong with Stephen, she answered with trepidation. Something was wrong with Stephen, all right, as Shelly soon learned from Richard, the male voice at the other end of the line. Shelly had met Richard on several occasions in large social gatherings, but she did not know him or his wife, Charlotte, well. Richard told Shelly that in recent months he had begun to be suspicious of his wife's behavior. He had just returned a day early (intentionally) from a conference only to find Stephen in bed with his wife. When he confronted the two of them, he asked Stephen, "Are you going to tell Shelly, or do I have to do it?" Stephen refused, thus the 2 A.M. phone call.

As the story unfolded, the affair had been in full swing before the move out of California. The move was all part of Stephen's master plan to get them out of a community property state, to isolate Shelly, be away from their new home a week at a time and be free to establish his new life.

Shelly nearly lost her soul's center and everything else. She was adrift. To all outside appearances, it looked like Stephen was "getting away" with all of his scheming and deceptive ways. Shelly felt betrayed, vulnerable, wounded and lost. Stephen had also been busy moving money around and burying assets. His actions were about as far toward "wrong action" as one could go.

Shelly would call me crying, "He's getting away with it!"

"No," I'd calmly reply, "it may appear that way today, but in the great and cosmic justice of life, he cannot get away with such wrong action." Then we would speak about karma, not from a revengeful view gleefully waiting for him to get his comeuppance, but from a knowing of the law of cause and effect. Our every action, no matter how small, is replete with consequences. Sexual activity that harms another person is never Right Action. It is pregnant with consequences. Through the ages sexual misconduct has created tremendous suffering.

Stephen's life is rife with consequences. Shelly just needed to be ever mindful that her hurt and anger did not fester into even more negative states that could manifest as more negative karma for her. She had much to examine and heal and forgive, before she could go on. Their divorce was long and further filled with deceptions. We kept speaking of her need to stand firm and not collapse under his raging intimidations and nasty behavior. It was very difficult, but she made it through. Shelly truly endeavored to practice conscious living even through her pain. She strove to be mindful of her actions and not succumb to rage that would mirror

Stephen's behavior. She is now living in California once again. She is practicing and studying Buddhist teachings, she is in the midst of intensive, ongoing counseling, and she is finding her center once again. Her suffering is coming to an end, in large part due to her Right Action. She is becoming happy once again. She is learning to forgive and trust herself.

This slice-of-life true story is an example of how all parties can suffer, how wrong action never brings good results or happiness, how in such troubling circumstances we can remember the noble Eight-fold Path and apply these methods as an antidote for whatever ails us.

A Buddhist view that I think is particularly helpful to one's spiritual growth is also to have compassion for Stephen, because a person such as he cannot behave so unskillfully unless he is already suffering greatly. Stephen may not immediately be aware that he is suffering, but in the ever constant flow of life he one day will see that such actions cannot bring him satisfaction or happiness. He will see that his unresolved inner conflict has caused him to suffer in the past, is causing him to suffer now and will cause him to suffer in the future. From a most enlightened perspective, compassion for him is called for.

Always keep your mind sublime and delight in sublime deeds.
All sublime effects come from sublime actions.

—*THE PRECIOUS GARLAND,*
CHAPTER 4, VERSE 9

When we obsess on another's faults and become consumed by them, we cause ourselves to suffer greatly and accomplish nothing. Our angry compulsion is like a toxic brew fermenting in our minds. We know people can do incredibly annoying things and have cruel behavior. Once I allowed a relative of mine to rob me of my peace of mind. He wasn't suffering (at least he wasn't aware of his suffering). I was suffering. After much spiritual practice, I finally was able to bless him and have compassion for him, freeing him from me and me from him. It was difficult and incredibly painful.

The law of karma is never suspended. No one ever lives outside its precise measurement. You live and act in accord with the truth of your being, or you pay the consequences. It's simple. It's exacting. It's true. You live life with Right Action, and the law of karma is forever blessing you.

Right Action follows Right View, Right Thought, Right Speech. When these three are faithfully engaged and practiced, Noble Action will naturally follow. How could the living of our lives be anything other than right, correct and true when we use Right View, when our thoughts are spiritually centered, when our speech is kind, accurate, loving and true? The questions have long been asked:

What do you do before enlightenment? Chop wood, carry water.
What do you do after enlightenment? Chop wood, carry water.

When my husband, David, and I were on a retreat at Thich Nhat Hanh's monastery, Plum Village, in Dordogne, France, among all our wondrous and deepening experiences was a terrifying one. It was a rainy and cold couple of days in mid-November. One afternoon I was quite sleepy and went to take a nap in our windowless, damp, concrete cell. About an hour later I was awakened abruptly by an American woman who breathlessly said, "There has been an accident, and David . . ." Before she finished my heart stopped and I felt all the blood drain from my head. Time froze.

When my consciousness finally returned to her, she was saying that a Canadian doctor was tending to him and that he would be okay. However, she added that we did need to take him immediately to the nearest clinic in this very rural area.

What had occurred was that David, being his helpful self, had been engaged in the classic Buddhist activity of what one does before enlightenment, chopping wood—literally. He was splitting hard oak logs, not a daily activity for David, an activity in which he had rarely engaged in his life. His impatience was growing, as the wood was not giving way easily to his ax. He had cut the first piece about halfway through when he thought he could move this tedious process along and break the log in two by slamming it into the concrete surface. He gave the log a mighty blow. It didn't break, but he was encouraged because he heard it crack. So he swung the log hard again, connecting with the concrete. This time, success ... of sorts.

The log broke in two, but the broken-off piece, jagged end up, bounced off the concrete and headed straight for his head. He said everything went into slow motion. He watched it heading for his left eye, but there was nothing he could do but duck a fraction of an inch. The jagged end missed his eye but smashed into his head just above the eyebrow, leaving a deep gash that bled profusely.

By the time I arrived, the Canadian physician had cleaned the cut, poured some antiseptic on it and applied a compress bandage. But she thought he needed stitches, so off we went to see a kindly French country doctor at his clinic. The doctor decided a special "American" bandage, not stitches, was needed, so that is what he applied, and David was repaired. The event ended well, and we forever had the answer to:

What do you do before enlightenment? Chop wood, carry water.
What do you do after enlightenment? Chop wood, carry water.

This dramatic tale points out what was intended to be an act of kindness and thoughtfulness also needed a hefty dose of wisdom to truly be Right Action. It certainly could not be called wrong action, because the intention was pure. It is just that impatience (ego) was given an opportunity to rise where wisdom (spirit) was what was called for.

While sitting in a teaching with His Holiness the Dalai Lama, my assigned seat was at a right angle to the Sangha where quite a few monks attentively sat. One monk was obviously responsible for a young tuka (what I lightheartedly call a "baby lama"). These are young boys who have been recognized as the reincarnation of a great lama of the past and are being mindfully trained, instructed and groomed to continue on with their previous life's mission—a very foreign concept to the Western mind, but a very important and ancient concept in Tibetan Buddhism. It is what occurred with the Dalai Lama at the tender age of two.

So this little boy, perhaps seven years of age, was in the front row across from me. He was more interested in his teacher's watch than what the Dalai Lama had to say. With his teacher faithfully focused on the leader of Tibetan Buddhism, the child unfastened the watch strap, took it off the monk and put it on himself. Then he reversed the process and returned the watch to the monk's wrist. He repeated this over and over and over. Once in a while the monk would look down and smile tenderly at the boy.

After perhaps two hours the boy took the watch off the monk and intentionally dropped it on the floor. With that the monk looked over, raised an eyebrow and extended his hand. The boy picked up the watch and placed it in the monk's hand. The monk refastened the watch on his own wrist and continued to listen to the teaching. The child then sat attentively for the rest of the presentation, quite unlike the behavior of most seven-year-olds.

This infinitely patient, kindly monk was Right Action personified. How many American parents would respond in such a way to a child? I think not many. I believe those living in accord with Right Action definitely walk gently upon the earth. They are mindful not to harm or to cause suffering to any creature.

In Japan on our honeymoon, David and I observed a father and his toddler son in a very similar exchange while sitting across from them on a train. The child, probably not yet two, would playfully put his tiny hand out the open train window and giggle. In turn, the father would patiently take the boy's hand and tenderly place it back inside the window. Just like the story of the young lama, this occurred repeatedly. The father demonstrated only loving-kindness, tenderness and patience. Again, Right Action in action. These small boys were tenderly loved and were never shamed or unnecessarily scolded.

What a contrast to the American mother I witnessed raging at her six-year-old son who was asking for a strawberry yogurt in a grocery store aisle. Wrong action. When I see such behavior, I always think, *twenty years of therapy*. This is not to be glib, but it is simply an observation, usually factual, after almost thirty years of ministry. To be infinitely loving and patient with a child is to instruct them in Right Action and to be life-affirming. To instruct them through yelling and harsh words and actions is life- and soul-robbing.

A most meaningful course to follow is to be aware enough of one's actions that no harm is done to any person or animal or any living thing. To live a conscious life we must be mindful of how our every action from the past and present impacts those around us and the environment. The words of the Dalai Lama come to mind: "When we are able to recognize and forgive ignorant actions of the past, we gain the strength to constructively solve the problems of the present."

Certainly all of us have acted in the past in ways we later regretted. Rather than living in that regret, we must practice forgiving ourselves for all mistakes and erroneous actions from the past. This process may take months, if not years, until we feel inwardly clear and free from the memories of our past mis-actions.

Through the years I have observed many individuals who have struggled deeply with learning how to apply the spiritual truths they study to the outer living of their lives. To live a life of spiritual balance, our actions must be an out-picturing of our spiritual study. To know truth principles intellectually but not to apply them to the moment-by-moment living of our lives is quite meaningless. As spiritual beings it is important that we embody the truth we know if our lives are to have true meaning, if we are to make a contribution to others.

A most effective way of doing this is to be certain that all our actions are in accord with our inner essence, being sure of that connection. Aware action (Right Action) is consistency of being. One way to express this consistency is to become the "observer of self." Learn to observe yourself, like you are viewing yourself in a movie, allowing your inner "I" to be silent. You witness your behaviors, views, thoughts, speech and actions. You examine how you speak to others on the telephone, to waitpeople, when you are annoyed with your partner or a child, when you are stressed, when you are running late and cut off in traffic. This is vital in one's journey of awakening.

Be the witness of your behaviors. Are you pleased with them? Or are you embarrassed or mortified with them? Would you say your actions in difficult situations are aware, are consistent with your inner essence?

If you are happy with your actions, fine. If not, you have work to do. If you have observed the need for improvement, bring forth consistency from within and without. That is the first step. The recognition that you need to work on aligning your actions with the truth of your inner nature is crucially important. Here is where transformation can begin to take place. Here you can begin to live in balance and correct your course of action when needed.

Expressing aware action is enormously freeing. It is truly a divine gift to live with a consistency between our inner consciousness and our outer expression. The more one can cultivate altruism for others, the greater blessings fall into one's own life.

The opposite of this is a selfish, self-centered view that leads to disturbing results.

To have a happy life, one must move out of self-serving interests and actions and endeavor to be a service to all without judgment or discrimination. Jesus taught that you can know true disciples by their fruits, by their actions. People can live out of a state of extreme self-centeredness, being so self-consumed that their thoughts and actions are always and only focused on self. These self-consumed ones truly have not learned to value others and realize their innate worth is just as precious as one's own. The Buddhists teach of learning to cherish others, a beautiful teaching. To learn to cherish others takes practice, constant practice. Here is an exercise to help you develop the capacity to cherish others:

Cherishing Others

Before arising, as you do your mental and spiritual preparation for the day, say to yourself something like this: "I know life is going to give me opportunities today to practice cherishing another. Let me be attentive enough to see the opportunity and to do something sensitive." The "something" may be to send a silent blessing or to give an extra-generous tip to a harried server. You could also attempt to kindly engage in a conversation with someone who is obviously having a troublesome day.

An effective way we can always cherish others is to have kindly thoughts about them, dropping any judgment or criticism, always giving them the benefit of the doubt. You do not need to search far and wide for individuals to cherish. Each day your living of life will put a few in your path.

In the recent past my husband and I were at a very tense baseball game. It would be a stretch to say that I'm a great fan, but a few times a year on a pleasant night a baseball game can be fun. This particular night we had fantastic seats, and the home team was shining. I had purchased a diet drink that came in an oversized cup. Each time I took a drink I placed the cup in the holder attached to the seat in front of me. I was focused on the game when the woman sitting to my left giggled and pointed at my cup. The man in the seat in front had stretched out his arm and allowed his hand and fingers to dangle over the side right into my cup!

The woman and I laughed. And I wondered, *What do I do?* Obviously no more of that soft drink would be consumed. A vendor came down the aisle yelling, "Cold beer, who wants a cold drink?" I thought, *I do.* For a moment I considered tapping that fan on the arm and asking him to buy me a replacement since four of his fingers were still in my cup. But I didn't do that, and I didn't say anything, knowing that whatever I said would be embarrassing to the man.

The purpose of life is to practice being a conscious individual, not causing another to suffer in any way. Telling that man his fingers were in my cup could have caused him a moment of suffering. So I didn't do it. And on that warm, autumn night, life gave me an opportunity to cherish a Cleveland Indians fan.

Our actions are the outer manifestation of the inner workings of our views, thoughts and speech. Right Action is conscious action. It is being so awake that we cease reacting to life and its challenges, and instead we are certain that our responses are conscious.

Do not waste your time in futile occupations.

—SOGYAL RINPOCHE

RIGHT LIVELIHOOD

EACH ONE OF THE POINTS on the Eight-fold Path is extremely important and is vital in interacting with the others. That being said, Right Livelihood is crucial. It is how most of us spend our waking hours. We all must find a way to earn our living to support our families and ourselves that is conscious. And it must be in alignment with these ideals. Our careers need to express loving kindness, integrity, service, compassion, generosity, equanimity, passion and joy.

Sergey Brin and Larry Page, veterans of a District of Columbia software company, created Google while they were idealistic Stanford University graduate students. The company still lists under "10 things Google has found to be true" that "you can make money without doing evil."

Right Livelihood is truly knowing you can earn a living and be prosperous without being a crook!

As a metaphysical minister for nearly thirty years, I surely know how deeply people want to be prosperous, to always have enough. We need enough money so that we can meet our needs and enough money to generously give and share. We need enough money so that money is not the focus of our lives. As Stuart Wilde, an Australian teacher of prosperity, says, "We need enough money so our lives are not a pain in the neck." If you have ever lacked financial wherewithal to adequately support yourself, never having enough to make ends meet, you know what suffering can be like. Financial lack certainly does not lead to liberation, rather from such a state one can harbor continuous feelings of discontent.

How much you need is totally up to you. You get to do the math. What that means is you can live consciously and work at a career you love, making a positive difference in the lives of others while prospering and experiencing financial ease.

Right Livelihood means having a career that does not harm yourself, others, animals, the environment or the future of our planet.

While writing this book, I met a young American who was a Zen Buddhist. While exchanging small talk, I asked what line of work he was in when he was not practicing at the Japanese Buddhist temple where we met. I am sure the shock in my eyes was not totally concealed when he told me he managed the slaughtering of animals at a nearby stockyard.

The Buddhists clearly state in their description of Right Livelihood that it shall not include "dealing in the meat trade." Perhaps this young man held the position before he became a Buddhist. Perhaps it was the only position available with a salary adequate to support his wife and children. I did not know, and I did not wish to judge. I knew in that moment that, if he truly desired to leave the stockyard due to his spiritual beliefs, there would be other opportunities available to him.

I am happy to report that serendipitously our paths crossed once again, and in the first few moments of our conversation he mentioned he had a new position. He is now employed by the county and engaged in work he finds most interesting and rewarding. *Right Livelihood.*

I loved the story of the eight coworkers from a meat-packing plant in Nevada who shared lottery winnings of more than $300 million. They all quit their jobs the same day they all became millionaires, an interesting and amazing way to leave a harsh career.

Sogyal Rinpoche states: "Don't waste your time in futile occupations." Many of us in our youth most likely had to engage in futile occupations. Several of these come to my mind, like a summer when I worked at Howard Johnson's. I earned almost nothing, and I was educated into the seed-ier side of life. It was about much more than scooping ice cream, and it was miserable. Ancient Buddhist teachings state that Right Livelihood must not transgress any of the Five Mindfulness Trainings that follow:

1. Dealing in arms. Owning a gun shop would be a no-no, as would be trading guns or weapons of any kind. About two months after the horrific Columbine incident, I agreed to fly to Denver to officiate at a wedding of some new friends. When I decided to leave the reception, I caught a ride back to my hotel from a wedding guest who was accompanied by her thirteen-year-old daughter. I had not met them until that evening. While chatting in the car, the daughter began to talk about a school outing the day before. It seemed that the children had created a reenactment of a historic battle, complete with muskets. In-stead of ammunition they fired flour at one another. If a child was "hit," he or she was declared dead and lay on the ground. I was in the backseat listening to this story, and I was horrified. Was this educational? Was this instructional? Was this benefi-cial? And it was, of all places, in Denver shortly after Colum-bine! Sadly the mother and daughter did not make the connection. When we are slumbering, we do not make the most obvious of connections. Children in Denver or anywhere should not, at a school outing, be playing at shooting and kill-ing one another. Some very troubled children grow up and transfer their games of childhood into violent activities of adulthood. I pray this book and these pure teachings assist peo-ple in making the connection—making the connection be-tween how we live our lives and what we think and how we act and what we say and what occurs in the outer manifestations of our lives. It is all connected, and we need to see it and live ac-cordingly. What will it take for us to collectively awaken?

2. Dealing in the slave trade. In our modern era the "slave trade" would be defined as anything that would cause another to be a slave—i.e., underpaying employees, investing in sweatshop businesses, taking advantage of young people, taking advantage of anyone. It would also be not recognizing that the minimum wage cannot adequately support one. It means dealing fairly with employees when you are their supervisor.

3. Dealing in the meat trade. This has always seemed gross to me as a non-meat-eater for most of my life, but I now know many spiritual types who eat meat, including Tibetan Buddhist monks. In their case the meat must be killed by someone other than themselves. (A Buddhist monk friend was explaining this to David, my husband, who replied that he could eat only living entities he could visualize killing himself. He could visualize catching and killing fish or clams, but not wringing a chicken's neck as he had seen his mother do when he was a child. Our monk friend thoughtfully considered what David said, and did not eat meat the rest of the time we were together.) I believe that on a soul level there is value to the kosher Jewish practice of how animals are slaughtered and which parts can be eaten.

4. The sale of alcohol, drugs or poisons. For generations my family members have owned and operated bars. I have been able to observe firsthand that in many circumstances this definitely could be viewed not as Right Livelihood. A close friend, Bob, whose family also owned bars, once observed, "It's not a clean business." And it's not. Awake people seldom hang out at saloons or taverns or make their livelihood from dealing in what for many is an addiction. Even though it is a legal job, one has to ask if it is the highest profession for one's soul.

5. Telling fortunes or making prophecies. My take on this is that dealing in the psychic realms, except for oneself, is not helpful

or desirable. (This prohibition is rather curious, however, considering that in Tibetan Buddhism there are those who are skilled at discerning signs and telling what the future will bring. And these individuals are highly regarded.) A contemporary interpretation would be to not make your living from another's neediness or vulnerability. The psychic realms surely exist, and the Buddhists address them and their aspects in various ways. So there is a place, but one who is gifted must be most mindful of how these gifts are used.

If we are currently engaged in a career that does harm any aspect of life or cause any suffering, we should pray and seek to find another more harmonious profession. Any job that involves killing, controlling others, cheating, selling controlled substances, sexual favors, making weapons, etc., is not Right Livelihood.

Right Livelihood could be expressed in an all-helping profession being of service, such as science, medicine, the arts, music, literature, publishing, painting, teaching, social work—any conscious business whose executives and support staff are dedicated to bringing forth ease, good harmony, love and understanding. Stephen Simon, the producer of the classic *Somewhere in Time* and the creator of an international spiritual cinema organization, is clear on his livelihood: "I came here to make movies," he stated succinctly while presenting a workshop at my church. And that is what he does.

JOE IS A professional undertaker and a friend who definitely practices Right Livelihood. He so consciously and lovingly does what for many would be very difficult work. He not only does it well, he does it masterfully. He gives full and mindful attention, not only to the family of the deceased, but to the deceased, as well.

When my beloved father passed on, I requested that we wait a week before my father's remains were cremated (in order to give the more subtle energies all the time necessary to exit the body). Joe not only understood but he lovingly agreed. He then went into the room where my father's body was being kept and spent an hour praying and meditating each day for my father on his journey through the Bardo (the Buddhist in-between state).

ONE THING of utmost importance I have learned in life is to be able to laugh at myself. If we step back and look at ourselves, we at times are very comedic in our thoughts and actions. Every summer I return to the coast of Massachusetts to the small fishing village where my family once lived. It is a place of refuge, the happy home of my childhood. It has a quieter pace than the city in which I now reside. I am inspired there, and I spend two to four weeks each year there writing. Most of the time I am alone.

One particular sunny afternoon I pulled into a gas station and began to look for a credit card when I became aware of someone staring at me. Looking at the driver's-side window there was a large, greasy young man peering in. I was startled. There was no one else around, and this fellow continued to stare at me, not going away. With fear gripping me around the throat, I reluctantly lowered the window one inch. "Yes?" I timidly croaked.

"Can I help you?" the rough-looking young man asked.

I temporarily screwed up my courage and queried in a stern voice, "With what?"

"With pumping your gas," he responded to this apparently daft woman. "Which grade?" he asked.

As the light slowly dawned, and before I could answer, I started laughing uncontrollably. It had been such a long time since I had been to a full-service gas station that I had thought this fellow was some type of marauder rather than a hardworking employee attempting to pump my gas for no extra charge.

I simply could not stop laughing at myself. When I finally gained control and explained my gales of laughter, he started to laugh, too. As we chatted, he told me how much he loved fixing cars, had left college early and was slowly buying this station from his uncle.

This young mechanic whom I had initially feared without cause was engaged, not only in mindful service, but in Right Livelihood.

Living consciously through one's life's work is to be a blessing to all whom you serve or who work for you. When one's work is not aligned with Right Livelihood, it will have far-reaching karmic consequences. We cannot live outside the law of Right Livelihood and long prosper. We may continue to make money, but we will not prosper in the truest sense of the word.

There is a function God has for each of us. And when we are living our holy function, we tremendously alleviate our suffering and are bringing about happiness in our lives and into the lives of all we touch.

"A noble person plans only noble things" (Isaiah 32:8). Living in accord with Right Livelihood results in one truly becoming a noble being. We all must endeavor to find that noble purpose and then live our lives prosperously in accord with love and compassion and understanding.

Right Livelihood is all of this and even more. It is enjoying your work and being fulfilled at the end of the day, rather than being on the verge of a stroke! It is bringing consciousness to every decision, answering yes to "Is this beneficial?" and no to "Is this harmful?"

Meditation is an important key to reach inspiration as to what career path conforms to Right Livelihood. If we are currently engaged in work that clearly is not Right Livelihood, then through meditation and prayer we can be shown how to change our course. We can find livelihood in a way that brings not only success to us but peace, as well, and plenty to all concerned.

Wrong livelihood pollutes the individual's consciousness, and that pollution in turn affects others, just as a toxin in water or in our food or in the air affects all who partake of it. Wrong livelihood can be for some alluring, because some see it as a means of getting rich. But in the greater

Right Livelihood Exercise

If you are examining your life and feel you are not living in accord with Right Livelihood, you have pinpointed the first of six steps helpful in correcting the situation:

1. Recognition.
2. Open yourself to new possibilities. Release any belief that what your work is now is all of which you are capable. Most folks think and live their lives in very narrow channels.

The partner of Elizabeth, a lifelong friend of mine, had a back injury at work (a job that required a great deal of physical labor) that laid him up for nearly a year. One evening on the phone Elizabeth was very stressed over the situation, telling me Leo had just returned from yet another medical evaluation and was told he had to remain off for another five to six months. He was also told he could never do work again involving any physical labor.

When I called back a few days later to check on them, Leo answered the phone. I did something quite uncustomary for me and said to him, "If I were your therapist, which I am not, or your minister, which I am not, I would say, 'Leo, the Universe is banging on your hood trying to get your attention. Find another non-physical occupation.'"

Leo was somewhat open to explore new possibilities, because his body simply could not support him returning to his former work as a housepainter. He is bright, artistic and talented, and he had been stuck in the idea that house painting was the only job he could do. He had to open to new possibilities.

3. Pray to be guided to your true career path, to be inspired. Quickly follow up on any inspiration that comes to you.

4. Lift your consciousness and vibrations to be a match for your new line of work.

5. Network with everyone you know. Let them know you are looking for a change.

6. Keep praying, meditating and visualizing and walk through the doors that are open. Recognize when the doors are closed, and walk through the new ones that open.

picture it is a path to suffering, lack and poverty, rather than riches. From the *Dhammapada*: "Don't try to build your happiness on the unhappiness of others. You will be enmeshed in a net of hatred."

When we are committed to living in Right Livelihood, our very commitment will draw to us the manifestation of our pure intention.

All the effort must be made by you;
Buddha only shows the way.

—*THE DHAMMAPADA*, VERSE 276

Right Effort

RIGHT EFFORT, SIMPLY STATED, is not dissipating your energy on the meaningless. Although all Buddhists (and I) believe in reincarnation, which they usually call "rebirth," we do not believe in wasting our energy in frivolous pursuits and mindless activity.

Once, a young acquaintance of mine complained bitterly how her live-in partner would spend endless hours at the computer playing games. They really had no relationship to speak of and did nothing together but split the rent and feed the cats. There was no glue to connect them physically or spiritually. Their relationship was shallow, and no amount of fussing with it was going to be beneficial.

Right Effort is thought of as Right Discipline or Right Diligence. There are four practices associated with Right Effort:

1. *Preventing unwholesome seeds to arise in us.* This is when we become so mentally aware that we can prevent unwholesome seeds in us to arise. They no longer have any place to live in our consciousness. This means we use our effort wisely, and we do not give our attention to that which is nonbeneficial, meaningless or the nonsense of life. We are actively engaging in the basic

spiritual law: "What we focus on expands." We are wise enough to guide our focus away from anything that would be unwholesome and no longer water seeds of ignorance, realizing that when we do, we are creating an ocean of suffering.

Think of your consciousness as a vast field into which many seeds have been sown. Good and wholesome seeds are already present in your field from the beginning of time. Unwholesome seeds have been scattered by two factors—your past and your present attachments. With every thought you think, with every breath you take, with every feeling you have, you are watering these seeds. You must learn to be mindful of what seeds you are watering. Ask: Are these the seeds that I want to grow? Do I want more feelings of hurt in my life? If no, then you have the power to stop watering seeds of hurt. Ask: Do I want more supportive friendships in my life? If yes, then be sure to water those seeds of loving and supportive friendship.

2. *Helping unwholesome seeds that have arisen to return to store consciousness.* We work with any of these seeds that are in our lives and stop watering them by withdrawing all our attention through our thoughts about them. We release the unwholesome seeds to the Holy Spirit, to Buddha or to bodhisattvas and consciously choose not to nurture them. This takes an enormous amount of effort and diligence. We must learn to say, "I will not give this my energy, my time or any of my attention." When done successfully, we can certainly call it "noble effort."

3. *Finding ways to water wholesome seeds in our store consciousness.* These are the seeds that have not yet borne fruit but that have been there since the beginning of time. We do this by knowing these good seeds are within us. We focus on what we do want, and it expands. We consciously water these seeds that are loaded with potential, and in time they begin to sprout and bloom. Even when you don't see the sprouting of the seeds, when they

are still "underground," it is important to continue to nurture and water them, just as you would a garden after planting seeds that produce beautiful flowers or succulent vegetables. When the tiny green growth of a tomato plant begins to sprout, you would not stomp on it, exclaiming, "This isn't what I expected! That's not a tomato!" Rather, you would know it was an early stage that was absolutely necessary for the full expression of the fruit of the tomato to come forth. So, too, we must continue to water those seeds of our spiritual potential until they are sufficiently matured to rise into full expression.

4. *Water wholesome seeds that have already arisen, so that they may continue to develop further.* In this Right Effort practice we focus on the manifest good, whereas in step 3 we were focusing on the potential good. Here we witness the sprout or even the full bloom, and we continue its nourishment through our thoughts, conversations, meditations, prayers and attention. We are clear in our focus. We hold the manifest good in our hearts and prayers. Our efforts are very good, and our diligence can be called "noble." These seeds are ready to bloom into even fuller expression.

Unwholesome seeds are seeds of grievance, greed, lack, ignorance, judgment, attack thoughts, fear, anger, revenge, criticism, hurt, etc. We must train ourselves to refrain from watering them. In our watering of seeds we do not ignore or deny the unpleasantness of life. But we do learn to properly deal with what needs to be dealt with in our lives and then to cease. We must let go of the negatives in our lives rather than attempting to hold onto them by continuing to water their negative seeds.

Wholesome seeds are seeds of love, peace, joy, loving-kindness, compassion, happiness, generosity, etc. These we must consciously water.

Right Effort is asking: Where are you putting your energy? Then you put it only in areas you want to grow. Remember, what we focus on expands. What we give our mental and emotional attention to we attract more of in life. Right Effort says expand only the good.

Where are you putting your attention in life? Put it only on that which you want more of in your life.

I cannot begin to count the number of people I have known who want to realize higher states of mind but do not want to do the work. They have wanted me or other spiritual teachers of theirs to do the work for them, and it just doesn't occur that way. As the Buddha said, "All the effort must be made by you." No one but you can have your breakthroughs, your "ahas." You cannot hire someone to do it for you. You must expend your time, effort and money.

Once during a question-and-answer session with the Dalai Lama, the question was asked, "What is the quickest, cheapest and best way to learn these teachings?"

Most of us in attendance were stunned at the question. The Dalai Lama put his sweet and gentle face in his hands and began to weep softly. The poignancy of the moment led my friend Linda and me to begin to fill with tears.

After several long moments, His Holiness once again sat up straight, took out his handkerchief, patted his eyes and wiped his glasses. When he finally spoke, you could have heard a pin drop. His response was, "This is not the question of a practitioner, for a practitioner would be willing to put all his effort, time and money into the pursuit of his spiritual path."

Then he told the story from his boyhood when he was not putting the proper amount of time and effort into his own meditative practice and was complaining a bit to his teacher. The teacher turned around, lifted his robe and exposed his bare bottom that bore two large calluses. How did the calluses get on his bottom? They got there from spending countless hours through the years sitting in meditation. It was quite a gripping story. *All of the effort must be made by you.*

So what is the quickest, cheapest and best way? There is no quickest, cheapest and best way!

Most Westerners fear the word or the concept of discipline. I have found it to be invaluable on the spiritual path—to be embraced rather than feared. Right Effort is allowing the truth to correct all errors in your mind. We cannot fail when we seek to reach the truth within us. So we embrace the idea of spiritual discipline, becoming like the wise disciples of the Buddha or Jesus. We do not run from the demands of our spiritual work. Rather we maturely embrace it and incorporate it into the moment-by-moment living of our lives.

Remember that the Buddha said that all the effort must be made by you. The power of diligence is yours alone. Right Effort is always remembering purpose, goal, mission, self. When Right Effort is engaged, how can our illusions satisfy us? Right Effort is knowing that the only sacrifice is to give up what has no reality. We can learn to be free of suffering, as the Four Noble Truths promise, and Right Effort is vital to attaining that end.

Living a life above the mundane, common human condition does take effort. It takes effort to choose the disciplined path. It takes effort to engage in one's spiritual practice daily, hourly. It takes effort to forgive. It takes effort to meditate several hours—or even twenty minutes—each day. It takes effort to not water the unwholesome seeds of grievances, lack, ignorance, victimhood, criticism, judgment, defensiveness and selfishness. And it takes effort to only water the wholesome seeds of love, caring, compassion, generosity, happiness and kindness.

Wise use of effort, diligence and care makes one aware of the basic nature of mind. Watering the wholesome seeds will always advance us on our spiritual path and lead us to living the noble life and revealing to us the true nature of mind.

Right Effort constitutes our systematic progress toward our goal of liberation. Before we extend any effort, it is good to ask: Is this to my or another's benefit? Is it a step leading to liberation, or is it going to lead to heartache, loss and suffering? Is it setting the course for nirvana or for samsara?

This is a great cosmic weather vane to use to decide if you are putting your energy toward leading to your ultimate happiness or to your ultimate suffering. Many a well-intended soul has gotten lost in samsara, that all-pervasive yet sometimes alluring state of the illusion, the dream.

I actually like the concept of samsara (the endless cycle of birth, life, death and rebirth) because it explains so much. And often it is quite helpful in making sense (at times) of just what the heck is going on. The advertisements of the world are constantly attempting to sell us on the splendor of samsara. Oh, how lovely this or that is, and how your life will be so much happier with the jewel of the moment. But, alas, it, too, will pass away. All the stuff of life could be called the samsara of life, for it does not lead to true joy but only future suffering.

An example of samsara would be any of the myriad addictions folks cling to and are consumed by. The addictive substance initially holds out the promise of pleasure and happiness, a promise that can never be kept for long.

All the allures of the world hold out a similar promise, but they, too, come up short. The tragic part is that we can sleepwalk through this life using all our effort, always seeking the elusive pot of gold and never finding it. And all the while the true treasure of gold lies within us, awaiting our realization and attention.

Please put your Right Effort into that which will lead to your watering the seeds of awakening and liberation and not getting caught in samsara.

*I think of mindfulness as the most effective
form of therapy and self-healing.*

—SOGYAL RINPOCHE

RIGHT MINDFULNESS

THE SIMPLEST DEFINITION of mindfulness for me is awakened attention. It is to be awake, aware, and to live as a conscious being. It also refers to deep meditation practice. When we embody mindfulness, our views are Right View, our thoughts are Right Thought, our speech is Right Speech, our action is Right Action, our livelihood is Right Livelihood, our effort is Right Effort, our concentration is Right Concentration.

We must be mindful in order to live the Eight-fold Path, to live a noble life as a noble being. To be attentive to mindfulness is to be attentive to the Christ within us, the Buddha within us, the Holy Spirit within us.

Right Mindfulness puts to the test the question: Is this helpful? This question I resonated toward upon first hearing it. It is like a reality barometer.

- Is this gossiping conversation helpful?
- Is this attitude helpful?
- Is this prejudice helpful?
- Is this fear helpful?
- Is this anger helpful?
- Is this guilt helpful?
- Is this lackadaisical attitude helpful?

- Is this long-held belief helpful?
- Is holding family secrets helpful?
- Is continuing to play the victim helpful?

Once at a workshop where my role was as a support person, rather than a leader, a very unpleasant situation erupted.

The participants were instructed to form a large circle around the room and to hold hands. One man refused to take the offered hand outstretched to him. When asked by the leader what was going on, the man's bold response in front of about fifty people was that he would not touch the hand of a homosexual. There was an audible gasp in the room. I felt shivers run over me as the leader exclaimed, "What? What are you talking about?"

The man, Oskar, raised in an Eastern European country, puffed himself up to defend his prejudice. "Bill said he is a homosexual, and I do not know where his hand has been, what it has touched." The tension in the room was palpable.

Bill quickly and consciously responded, "I'll move." And he did, but not because of the man's prejudice, upside-down thinking or unskilled behavior. Bill did not take the event personally. I was very proud of Bill and the attitude he displayed. Oskar needed help to look at a long-held belief system that did not serve him. It was not helpful.

A break soon followed in which I found Oskar, a former counselee of mine, pacing like a caged animal outside the workshop room. I asked if he wanted to talk about what had just happened inside. He immediately began to defend his position, and I tried to steer the conversation in a more "helpful" direction. I asked him to tell me about his experiences with gay men, and he replied that he had never known a gay man before. His comment made me stifle my laughter at its absurdity. "How is that possible?" I asked.

Oskar replied, "There are no gay men in my country. Homosexuals are dirty, and I have always been taught that if I ever met one, I should have nothing to do with him." I responded that, whether he knew it or not, he had met dozens if not hundreds of homosexual men in his life. They are not inherently dirty. And, yes, they do live in his country, most certainly closeted, but there nonetheless. Bill's hand had not touched anything his own hand hadn't touched. AIDS does not leap off the body of a homosexual, and Bill doesn't have AIDS. I asked where his terribly misguided belief had arisen. He again defended his belief system, saying it was what he had always been taught.

I recalled the song from the musical *South Pacific* that includes the line "We have to be taught to hate, carefully, carefully taught." Throughout his life Oskar had been carefully, carefully taught to hate gays. Knowing his response in advance, I asked him if he had ever examined his belief system and explored if his rigid attitudes were beneficial to his life. "No," he said. "Why should I? They are true. They are what I have been taught."

However, after a lengthy conversation, Oskar became willing to look at his programmed beliefs and to begin questioning their validity. I asked him to keep exploring the question "Is this helpful?" In a private appointment several days later Oskar began to admit that, no, this attitude was not helpful, kind, loving or who he wanted to be.

Mindfulness is awakened attention. When we are mindful we notice everything. A very humorous personal story occurred at the Pilates studio I frequent three or four times a week. This is not a sangha where one goes to meditate and discuss philosophy with no regard for the body. It is a small space with its whole emphasis and reason for being focused on the physical.

Before joining this studio I had gained a great deal of weight during a time of burning grief. From my normal size eight I had ballooned to a full twelve. So I began attending several times a week working with several personal trainers. All my sessions were private.

After a year of gaining strength and muscle tone, I was ready to shed the excess baggage. And almost no one noticed when I did! Ten pounds. Okay. Not much difference, except to me. Twenty pounds. Nary a comment. Thirty, forty, fifty pounds. No comments. One coach did notice, and she and I made a game of wondering when one of the other trainers would notice. It took eight months! This was eight months of seeing me at least three times a week. If I had gone from 400 pounds to 350 pounds, I could understand. But I looked much, much smaller.

Right Mindfulness is noticing what is going on right in front of our eyes and ears. We notice the presence, energy and essence of a loved one. How is she doing? How does she look—content, happy, sullen, blue? How does his voice sound? How is his speech—excited, flat, engaging, distant? When we are mindful, we not only notice, we care. A mindful person is an aware, caring, kind, loving person. They give conscious attention to others.

I admire best-selling author Wayne Dyer and his mindfulness. My church has brought him to Cleveland a number of times. After each of his speaking engagements, he will stand for hours warmly greeting every one of his supporters. I have long noticed how he gives each person his total, undivided attention. Very impressive! Most mindful!

We can all live mindfully as we make the effort to become more aware and awake to ourselves and others. Then it truly can be said that we are living a noble life. The first meditative practice I was taught was Mindfulness Meditation. When I look back at those thirty years, it is so amazing that I was given the teaching, since I didn't know at the time its significance and life-altering effect on my future and continued relevance to this day.

MINDFULNESS MEDITATION EXERCISE

My initiation into meditation came with being taught how to relax the body, sit in a stable position and bring the fullness of attention upon the breath. One monitors the breath, being fully aware of the rising and falling of the chest with each breath.

Begin breathing in mindfully.

Breathing out mindfully. Silently say, *I am aware of my breath.*

Say silently with each inhalation and exhalation: *Breathing in. Breathing out.*

Do this very slowly and most mindfully, bringing your total awareness into what you are doing, observing each breath as it rises and falls. Silently say, *Rising, falling,* as you go deeper and deeper into the meditation with each passing minute.

The Vietnamese Zen master teacher Thich Nhat Hanh uses the endearing term "mouth yoga" to help describe this mindfulness practice that brings one into the present moment.

In, out.

Deep, slow.

Calm, ease.

Smile, release.

Present moment, wonderful moment.

It is most precious to consider this technique as yoga for our mouths and lungs.

Mindfulness meditation is just that—becoming fully mindful during one's meditation. This technique is so simple and yet so powerful. Faithful, daily practice of it can change your life. I've done it for three decades and still simply love it and its effects on my mind, body and soul.

Practicing Mindfulness Meditation brings our whole life and the other seven aspects of the wheel into balance. It supports Right View. It clarifies our thinking into Right Thinking. Right Action follows a time of sitting meditation. It leads us into our correct career, Right Livelihood. It makes all of our efforts rewarding through Right Effort. Right Mindfulness goes hand in hand with Right Concentration and deepens all of our spiritual practices.

Don't wait to begin to practice until you have the feeling it is time to do so. It may be too late. Sadly I have often witnessed this happen. Many people only turn to a spiritual practice and prayer when they are facing desperate circumstances. When the fifteen-year-old daughter is pregnant; when the husband is having affairs; when you are sick, tired, stressed, feeling empty inside; when you feel life has lost not only its luster but any meaning, and you feel overwhelmed. It may be too late.

I believe the greater truth is that it is *never* too late for any of us. But the longer we remain disconnected in consciousness from our spiritual core, the more overwhelming the circumstances of our lives seem to us. They push upon us from all directions, and we can feel helpless, hopeless, void of any resources.

But the good—no, great—news is that at any moment we can begin to live mindfully. We can wake up and take a life-affirming step in a positive direction. We can begin to utilize these extraordinary tools. These eight principles are unparalleled in the annals of spiritual philosophy and teaching.

If we are mindful, we will never wait. And when a challenge arises, we are already prepared. We are not adrift upon a sea of discontent and discord. We are anchored to our spiritual core.

There is an antidrug campaign slogan, "Parents, the antidrug." I add to that, "Mindfulness, the antidrug." If parents were truly mindful of their children's spiritual well-being, activities, friends, school and teachers, transportation and just where they were, how could there be a drug problem?

To varying degrees I have been part of hundreds of families' lives. With the possible exception of an emotionally disturbed child or a child carrying an enormous load of negative karma, spiritually centered, emotionally healthy, loving and compassionate parents raise spiritually whole and healthy children. What children need is love and attention—not more techno toys, computers and TV time. To have healthy children, they must be the priority. The family must be the priority.

Sara, a top stockbroker in Cleveland, is a neighbor of ours. She and her husband have five children, and they have miraculously managed to raise amazing kids. They are the type of children who love one another and seem to do everything they do in an exceptional fashion. I am in awe of this family.

The children attend parochial schools and have all the usual extracurricular activities: music lessons, basketball, aerobics, baseball, chess, etc., etc. But the number one priority for this family remains the family.

When Sara is asked by top clients to have an evening meeting, a dinner meeting, a Saturday meeting, she always graciously declines by saying, "I'm so sorry, but that's my family time."

Sara often gets an astonished inquiry from a client. "Well, how often does your family have dinner together, given your busy lifestyle with so many varying schedules?"

Her somewhat incredulous response, a favorite of mine, "Oh, we have dinner together every night."

Parents are the antidrug, the anchors of light and love for their children.

Living mindfully is always beneficial to the entire household. When we are mindful we notice if our cat or dog is suffering, if our car needs attention, if the roof needs repair. Mindfulness is a very deep practice, but it is also a very practical practice.

Mindfulness allows us to look deeply into our conscious and subconscious minds. The Buddhist term for "subconscious mind" is "store consciousness." We must look deeply into store consciousness, where all the seeds of our beliefs are stored.

It took much coaching to get Oskar to be willing to look into his "store consciousness." The store consciousness of Sara, her husband and children is that of love, deep familial connections, genuine caring for one another. For the children these beautiful seeds in their store consciousness must serve them in ways yet to be realized as they and their seeds mature and blossom.

As you become a more mindful being, always remember the beautiful seeds you are planting in your store consciousness. If there remains within old decaying seeds that would never serve your growing awareness, be willing to incorporate all the techniques and exercises to cleanse yourself, so your mind can be purified in order for you to begin to live a future far more rewarding than the past. The Buddha's glorious teachings only point the way. All the effort must be done by you.

TONGLEN MEDITATION

Tonglen, a remarkable meditation practice, literally means giving and receiving. Tonglen opens our hearts in a way unlike any other practice. It opens us to others in a way that allows us to be truly present to them and their suffering. We no longer fear another's pain, but rather we reach out to them in their time of deepest need.

Tonglen is multifaceted, for as it teaches us to be compassionate and assist in alleviating another's suffering, it is also unparalleled in working on our egos—at the root of all of our own suffering. The practice of Tonglen can transform us into masters of compassion. For those so dedicated, this takes many years and much practice.

For me the practice of Tonglen is a very deep mindfulness practice, for it engages our whole awareness and entire being. We practice Tonglen truly caring for others as we would desire to be cared for.

The practice of Tonglen should only be undertaken by those with some degree of spiritual maturity and some mastery of meditation. The reason for this is that it is such a selfless practice that for the uninitiated the ego could definitely rise during this highly focused meditation and cause all manner of soul mischievousness as we fully open ourselves to the suffering of others.

The practice of Tonglen is so powerful that from the eleventh century, when the Buddhist teacher Geshe Chekhawa began teaching it to a few lepers, they practiced it faithfully and were cured of their leprosy. Word spread of this remarkable practice that could cure an incurable disease nine hundred years before the medical discovery of sulfone drugs.

An interesting and amazing tale is told of the practice of Geshe Chek-hawa that occurred near the end of his life. Apparently in his deep compassion, with his burning desire always to be of help in alleviating others' suffering, he unceasingly prayed to be reborn in what the Buddhists call the "hell realms." We can all probably conjure up an image of a hell realm and probably have all hung out there a number of times.

Geshe Chekhawa prayed such a prayer, not because he was a masochist, but because he was close to becoming a saint and wanted to be of assistance to all those living and suffering in the hell realms. He was disappointed when his dreams revealed to him that he was to be reborn into one of the realms of the Buddhas. This deeply saddened him, and he asked his student to pray that this would not occur! His incessant desire was to be of help to those who are suffering in hell realms.

When I first learned of this tale, I could hardly believe it. I was alternately crying and laughing, thinking surely in lifetimes past this must have also been my prayer, for it would so tidily explain the mystery of my own personal times of tremendous suffering. Perhaps in ages past I, too, had prayed to be of soul benefit for those who would suffer in the future. If that be the case, I now choose to change my prayer, plant new seeds and pray that we can all be transformed to be reborn in one of those beautiful Buddha realms.

The Tonglen Technique

You first evoke the greatest amount of love and compassion you possibly can within you. Recall the times in your life when you have felt the greatest love being given to you. Thankfully through grace we have all been loved deeply, if not long, at least once. We need to reclaim that memory from a parent, grandparent, lover, aunt, cousin, sibling, teacher, minister or neighbor. I am very fortunate to feel and know I have been loved by both my parents. It is the love of my father that continues to feed my soul and spirit, even though he is now physically gone. Find that great love of your soul and allow that feeling to fill every aspect of your being.

Breathe love in and out deeply. Allow your chest to rise and fall with your heartbeat of love. Allow that feeling of great love to wrap itself around and through your heart like a warm blanket. Sense a deep gratitude in knowing you have been so loved and are now capable yourself of loving.

Begin to visualize opening your heart, as your enormous love is directed outward to enfold other beings. You can do this for one person, or a family, or your sangha, or for all beings who are suffering with a particular illness or state of being. Now you bring them into this love within your heart. Tonglen is different from many meditative practices in that you are not sending your subjects this great love. Rather, you are bringing them *into* this great love.

My dear friend Suzanne practiced Tonglen as she went through radiation and chemotherapy for breast cancer. She engaged in it several times daily, bringing joy into her meditation to all women currently facing the same diagnosis and similar follow-up treatment after surgery. We know it helped other women, and it is definitely beneficial to Suzanne.

The Tonglen practice can be extended to all, even those who are most difficult and challenging for us. Begin to see that difficult person as one who is suffering just as you have suffered, and in doing so you feel compassion for him awakening in you. You shall then begin to see how similar you are. I do think it is helpful to do what one early teacher of mine taught. Begin with those you already love and who love you before you move on to other, more difficult ones.

As one advances in the practice of Tonglen, it takes on a powerful characteristic of no longer seeing the person as other, but now as same. In our minds we exchange our sense of self with whatever the other person is suffering. Her pain becomes your pain. And you can do something about it. You can actually learn to dissolve the pain or affliction within your own heart space. One way to do that is to see it as a ring of heavy, dark clouds encircling your mind, swirling around you. Know that beyond the denseness of the clouds, which represent suffering, lies love, compassion, freedom, transformation and light. Then visualize the great love within you as so enormously powerful that you can easily with the simple sweep of your hand brush those heavy clouds aside. As you do so, the light that lies beyond them begins to dissipate the clouds into vapor and then into nothingness. You now realize, through the Tonglen practice, that you can move completely through the illusion of suffering. It can produce outstanding results benefiting both the one suffering and you.

Exchanging yourself for others is extremely powerful and is not to be undertaken by spiritual lightweights. The energy is simply too powerful and too demanding.

Another way of evoking compassion to practice Tonglen is to call upon an illumined being, be it Jesus, the Buddha, the Divine Mother, Tara or a bodhisattva. Then feel the boundless love that being has for you. Sink deeply into that love and absolutely know that it is real. Now channel that great reservoir of love to the focus of your Tonglen practice. Hold him in the love and for as long as you can maintain the intensity of that profound love.

An essential component of all phases of Tonglen, as taught to me by Lama Chonam, is to take the other's suffering into your heart space. In most Western healing practices the heart energy is sent out to the recipient. In this Buddhist practice the recipient is brought into your own heart. Herein lies the contrast between the Western and Eastern mind.

This one aspect is what makes Tonglen so powerful and not for the immature on the spiritual path. One has to be quite clear to be engaged in such a high level of spiritual work and actually take pain and suffering, which we normally try to avoid, into our very hearts.

Practicing Tonglen and core mindfulness meditations is never enough. We must rise up from the meditations and live our lives mindfully with our family in our homes, with our friends, in our work environment with our coworkers, on our highways, in society, with our consumption of resources, with our own thoughts and minds. Then our entire lives can be transformed and we become mindful beings. We become the noble ones, the ones lost in the wonder of compassion and delight. Like His Holiness the Dalai Lama, we start to giggle at the overwhelming delight of living an awakened life.

Mindfulness opens our eyes and ears to the beauty and wonder of life. Here we can love and be compassionate in the present moment . . . and it is a wonderful moment.

The following is a Tonglen practice that I was given after 9/11. I do not know where it came from or who assembled it. With that in mind, I respectfully share it with you:

Tonglen—A Tibetan Prayer Practice

Breathe light in and out of our hearts. Just breathe ever so deeply, as deeply as you can, and release.

We breathe in and focus the totality of our attention to our heart center.

We breathe out, seeing your heart now as a vast orb of intense love moving to your heart chakra, that has remained undisturbed,

And expanding consciously, mindfully, dynamically your heart energy with every breath.

Pushing the energy out a bit further and allowing it to contract only to expand with the next breath

Holding only love.

Being ever so still, perfectly still.

In the depths of your heart, love is awakening.

Levels of love, levels of being that perhaps have been resting for a very long time.

They have not been called into action, into response until now. Breathe into our hearts, love.

Until you can imagine your heart center not just being in the center and slightly to the left,

That your heart center begins to fill your whole chest area, extends out before you, in front of you.

Extends behind you, rising up to your throat, down to your navel. This whole area becomes a warm pulsating center of love and light.

And now we are called to bring into our hearts, images of the recent tragic events of Tuesday, September 11th.

Bring into our hearts these images and to allow this love to just infuse them,

Transform them from pain into peace, from a desperate lost energy into one faith.

Let us first bring into our hearts those whose lives were so swiftly ended on Tuesday.

Those on the planes, those in the World Trade Center. We bring those individuals into our hearts.

Perhaps some have lifted into the infinite and perhaps some are in the state of confusion.

We bring them, those especially, into our heart center. We breathe in the light, breathe peace.

And very mindfully we breathe out the trauma. We are willing to do this work for them.

This is how great our love is.

Breathe in that shock, that horror.

Breathe it out, breathe love into their souls that they be lifted in peace now, into the infinite. That we and they know together that life is eternal.

So we let them go and bring into our hearts their family members. We've seen them, heard their stories.

We've seen their anguish and incredible grief.

We are courageous enough, as spiritual beings, to bring their pain into our hearts.

And to allow this enormous love that we have to begin to burn away that pain, to dissolve that pain, to transform that pain, transform that suffering and sense of loss, bewilderment.

If your heart gets very heavy, very intense, just really emphasize the exhalation.

Breathe that energy out.

Just pour out immeasurable love into the lives of these beings. If we think that this is an impossible task, we need to remember the words of A Course in Miracles: "How long is an instant?"

We continue on.

We release these loved ones, and welcome into our heart centers now the firefighters, policemen, the heroes that don't want to be called heroes.

We bring them into our heart and we send them boundless love, immeasurable gratitude.

We let the shock that they have been through, the devastation that they have witnessed, be dissolved into our heart centers now.

Energy is moving in this room, grace is being sent forth.

Bring into our hearts, those that were in or near the building that escaped,

How they must be wrestling with gratitude and regret and confusion.

We bring all those emotions that they must be experiencing into the powerful space of our committed hearts.

We bring that energy in, that they may be consoled, that we may be the ones to console them, that they may know peace, that they may know that there is an order at work that one day they may understand.

Bring all of their conflicted emotions, courageously, bravely, into our own hearts and let that energy be burned off by the all-consuming energy of our heart centers.

Breathe in ever so deeply.

Bring into our hearts those that lost part of their world, which would really be every one of us.

Our hearts are large enough to contain this. We are one, one in the heart of God.

We let the all-consuming love of our hearts transform this energy as well.

Now our hearts are so enormous, our love is so limitless, that we now bring in those that have been the perpetrators, those that have hated us, those that have judged us so harshly. Very gently, easily we bring this energy into our hearts.

We allow it to be dissolved, to become nothing, for it is not the reality of their beings.

Let that energy be dissolved in our hearts now.

We are like the spiritual surrogates, so committed to the path of healing, of transformation, that in this very room, this very moment, miracles are being created.

We breathe this energy in and breathe it out, being ever so sure to breathe all that energy out.

And then we are simply together in the silence for a moment. We know there is nothing our Holiness cannot do.

Say it to yourself, "There is nothing my Holiness cannot do."

We are a blessing unto the world.

Doing these various Tonglen practices will be an enormous blessing to others, many of whom you will never meet, and in its practice you, like Geshe Chekhawa, will be growing in compassion.

*When you do reenter everyday life, let the wisdom, insight,
compassion, humor, fluidity, spaciousness and detachment
that meditation brought you pervade your
day-to-day experience.*

—SOGYAL RINPOCHE

RIGHT CONCENTRATION

IN 1973 I WAS first exposed to Buddhist meditation practices. My young
mind (or "beginner's mind," as Buddhist teaching would call it) took
to meditation, as the saying goes, "like a duck to water."

Soon after that I became the "subject" in biofeedback meditation pre-
sentations. A number of electrodes were hooked up to my head, and in a
few minutes I would slip from outer awareness (beta) into inner stillness
(alpha). Then I would go much deeper (theta). I always remained conscious but totally detached from any outside stimulation such as sounds
or noises or temperature changes. At such times part of my mindfulness
meditation training was to silently repeat, *Sounds, sounds, I am hearing
sounds.* Then I would consciously breathe in and breathe out, returning
full focus to my breath. I was a real "whiz kid" of meditation. As I look
back on those days, it seems I brought that energy and knowing with me
from previous lives, because I so easily and quickly went into such deep
meditation.

Practicing Right Concentration is to cultivate a mind that is "single-pointed." The initial form of meditation I was engaged in is called "active concentration." There one observes in a very detached manner whatever presents itself and then lets it go and refocuses on the breath—always returning to the present moment, the now.

The second aspect of Right Concentration is "selective concentration." You choose one object and direct your full focus on it. The object could be a flame, a flower or a deity.

The more skilled we become in our meditation practices in Right Concentration, the more enriched our lives become, the happier we become. For nearly 2,600 years hundreds of thousands of monks and nuns have spent their lives solely dedicated to their spiritual practices. What evolved were certain formulas, such as meditations, that we can take and superimpose on our present spiritual understanding and practices and receive consistent results.

The first time I attended a teaching of the Dalai Lama was 1991 at Madison Square Garden in New York City. During a question-and-answer time, he was asked the question: "How long should we laypeople meditate daily—not the monks and nuns—but the average American practitioner?"

His Holiness reflected on the question for several very long moments and then responded, "Four hours, four hours would be good."

There was an audible gasp that rose from the nearly four thousand attendees. At that time I made an inner commitment to meditate two hours a day. On only a few occasions have I spent four full hours in meditation within a twenty-four-hour day. Four hours is a very long time. Two hours is a very long time. If you are a newcomer to meditation, don't even attempt two hours, because in all likelihood you will grow weary and quit, probably after only a few days. And that is not the goal.

Since that time in New York I have endeavored to meditate two hours daily. People ask me how that is possible since I have such a full life. At least one to one and a half hours is dedicated to Right Concen-

THE LOTUS STILL BLOOMS · 83

tration during the night. Not sleeping through the night does not mean counting sheep. Counting breaths and mantras can be far more beneficial.

At those times of life where there has been just too much on my plate and my meditation has suffered, I have suffered. I have learned I simply cannot let "life" press in on my time of solitude of which I require a lot. Without Right Concentration life simply does not work well for me. It is reported that Gandhi would rise between 3 and 4 A.M. and silently meditate to prepare for his full schedule. He considered this his most important act of the day, since it gave him the energy to do whatever would come before him. Charles Fillmore, cofounder of the Unity movement, would arise in the middle of the night and spend extended times in meditation. There is something quite sacred about the stillness of the predawn hours. Interference from the fast-paced, frenetic world with all of its bombardment from disruptive waves of ego has not yet begun, and one can more easily relax into the quiet.

In reflecting on the eight points of the Eight-fold Path, it is clear that I began my practice of them with Right Concentration. This is not the norm. Usually one starts with Right View or Right Thought, the preliminary aspects that are essential. These two are followed by Right Speech, Right Action and Right Livelihood. These three align the living and expression of one's life with the ideal. The final three—Right Effort, Right Mindfulness and Right Concentration—are developmentally advancing one toward the goal of spiritual understanding and awakening.

Right Concentration is not to be used as an escape mechanism. That would be wrong concentration. Rather, Right Concentration builds the consciousness for us to live deeply with clear awareness each moment of our lives.

Following are several concentration practices that I have used and taught through the years.

Falling Leaves

This exercise will take you twenty to thirty minutes.

- First, in a quiet place sit either on the floor in a yoga posture or in a chair with your spine straight, feet flat on the floor, hands in a relaxed, open, palms-up position.
- Then still your mind by breathing in and out slowly with awareness. Do this for several minutes until you feel yourself becoming inwardly quiet.
- Next imagine ten leaves gathered in the region of your third eye (the center of your forehead). They are your leaves. Choose whatever kind you wish. One student of mine actually gathered leaves in the autumn and placed ten of them on a tray in front of her. She would look at the leaves, close her eyes, visualize the leaves, once again open her eyes, look at the actual leaves, close her eyes again and begin the concentration practice. She reported that this technique was very beneficial for her. Awaken your creative imagination and find a way that would inspire and be beneficial to you.
- Now with each breath imagine a single leaf floating from your forehead to your solar plexus. Stay very centered and focused in your concentration. Do this until all ten leaves are resting in the solar plexus without experiencing distracting thoughts.

This takes a great deal of concentration, so do not get discouraged. Do not judge your efforts. Be kind and gentle to yourself, as if you were training a new puppy. Keep the practice joyful and light-spirited. Do not stress or strain. Refrain from getting exasperated. Allow this to be a pleasurable experience. After several weeks of practice, Right Concentration combined with Right Effort will create the ability in you to do a complete set of ten without distraction. The Buddhists say that, when one can do ten sets of ten, then that person is beginning to master Right Concentration. I personally used this technique daily for a very long time while training my "beginner's mind."

I encourage you to practice daily the leaf meditation, and when you feel a degree of mastery, then move on to more complex mindfulness techniques such as the ones at the end of this book. You do the work, and it will work for you. Faithfully continue in your practice and in time you will reap the priceless benefits to your inner being. Remember to be certain you are not sitting quietly with your eyes closed thinking about anything—no to-do list, no balancing the checkbook, no worrying about anything. If you are, refocus your attention on your breathing:

In and out, rising, falling, peace within, peace without, calm within, calm without.

If you need more practice with concentration, then revisit those ten leaves. You are worth the time and effort. Your soul is worth the time and effort. The time spent developing Right Concentration will return to you blessed many times over.

Walking Meditation

This exercise can take thirty minutes to an hour or more. My husband and I became somewhat skilled in walking meditation while on retreat at Plum Village in France with Thich Nhat Hanh.

In the French countryside Thich Nhat Hanh would very mindfully and most slowly walk with his eyes looking neither right nor left, cast slightly downward. Imagine the scene with this diminutive monk leading seventy-five adults and a few children single file in the slow, nearly motionless walk with French farmers driving by in their tractors or horse-drawn carts gaping at the unusual spectacle in their bucolic land. A mischievous, impetuous little boy, who was the son of parents in our group, would run in front of Thich Nhat Hanh flailing his arms in an attempt to distract the teacher. The child never succeeded. Thich Nhat

Hanh remained composed, mindful and centered in spite of the child's antics.

This is a lovely practice that aligns the physical body and its motion through centering, purposeful movement. It also has the benefit of stilling the mind. Try it on a quiet beach or park or forest. It is very beneficial. David and I always lead this walking meditation when we lead group retreats in Hawaii, and we silently walk mindfully single file through a pristine ironwood forest. The ironwoods sway and creak in the breeze. It is as if the gentle sounds of their vibrations are communicating peace to us. The single-file line of retreatants slowly moving through the forest is gradually enveloped by the oscillations of the trees. It has always been a very meaningful experience for all.

Sitting on the Car Meditation

This is another meditation that focuses on Right Concentration that I learned and practiced at Plum Village. We signed up for "Sitting on the Car Meditation," which, when I read the title, made me burst out laughing as I visualized many Buddhists using Right Concentration mindfully sitting all over the cars in the small parking lot. It was quite a comical mental image.

As it turned out, something was lost in translation, for it was supposed to read "Sitting *in* the Car Meditation." But the correct translation hardly helped, for what it really meant was piling sixteen to seventeen people like sardines into an old van, where we were to be silent as the Vietnamese driver wove us through the French countryside, transporting us to our intended destination. It was an attempt to remain centered while wrapped around the gearshift! I would silently practice mindful breathing or count my Tibetan mala beads to remain focused, centered and calm.

Riding so squeezed into a vehicle with others I do not recommend, but we can always bring mindful concentration to our driving, whether alone or with passengers. What happens to drivers in stressful situations is quite revealing as to what lurks in "store consciousness" (the Buddhist term for the subconscious mind). It must be one of my soul lessons, because on several occasions I have been the passenger of drivers who are spiritual practitioners, but who—when they encounter a hostile driver on the road—quickly match negative energies, cursing and swearing and making rude gestures. Such behavior is not worth it.

Calm in, calm out, peace in, peace out.

The highways of life will always be filled with unskilled drivers. Another's driving skills need to have nothing to do with our maintaining calm at our spiritual center. A helpful technique to remind you to remain in your center is to print cards with calming phrases such as "Sitting in the car meditation," "Breathe," or "Calm in, calm out," and tape them to your dashboard. Some place a picture of a much-loved saint or teacher, or they hang mala beads over the rearview mirror. If you find you can easily lose your spiritual equilibrium while driving, why not incorporate one or more of these ideas?

Practicing Right Concentration in one's car can be both a safety and a centering device for drivers and passengers alike. If all drivers practiced an outer-directed Right Concentration while behind the wheel, what an impact it would have for us all as road rage and accidents began to disappear.

RIGHT CONCENTRATION in its higher state is to become absorbed in one's meditative practice from moment upon moment without disturbances or distractions. As with the other seven points on the wheel, Right Concentration must be combined with all the others, especially Right View and Right Effort. It is reported that there are those who have sat in meditation for years, or so they thought, but their practice truly was not Right Concentration or Right Effort. Although they sat, they were always distracted or worried or planning their day. Therefore they were never actually meditating. This is where, in the early stages of my practice, working with biofeedback proved to be so beneficial. The reading from the monitor to which I was hooked up gave continual feedback as to whether I was actually in a meditative state or simply sitting quietly with my eyes closed and making out a shopping list.

Right Concentration takes years of spiritual practice to begin to gain any degree of mastery. The years of effort are so worthwhile because of the peace, compassion and insight into the nature of mind that it brings.

Practice these simple Right Concentration techniques faithfully by incorporating one or more into your daily practice, and you will begin to notice the transformation of your mind and a great inflow of peace.

Don't let yourself be slack, but don't stretch yourself to break
either. The middle course, living between too much and
too little is the way of the Eight-fold Path.

—THE BUDDHA

The Middle Way

THE MIDDLE WAY is achieved when one reaches that point of cosmic balance between austerity and the creature comforts of the world. The ascetics who were with the Buddha were critical of him because he was no longer living an austere lifestyle. They considered his life too "cushy." He was eating beautiful food and wearing a fine robe, while they existed on a few grains of rice and slept uncovered on a bed of nails.

The ascetics asked the Buddha, "What kind of teacher and yogi are you? You are soft, weak, indulgent."

To which the Buddha replied, "I, too, have slept on nails; I've stood with my eyes open to the sun in the hot sands beside the Ganges. I've eaten so little food that you couldn't fill one fingernail with the amount I ate each day. Whatever ascetic practices under the sun human beings have done, I, too, have done. Through them all I have learned that fighting against oneself through such practices is not the way."

Through the years I have known a few ascetic type personalities who forever deny the body, its needs and its care. One young man I knew was so physically beautiful and so unhappy and grim. His eating habits were very austere and unpleasant. He always seemed to be miserable in the pursuit of his spiritual awareness. He munched on raw garlic cloves like they were peanuts and insisted they left no pungent odor on his breath. The rest of the world did not agree. I recall one acquaintance saying to this fellow that he would probably throw himself under a train rather than eat a Frito. His response was, "What's a Frito?" If misery, self-denial and self-imposed suffering were the way to get "it," we would all have gotten "it" a long time ago.

The Buddha emphasized the Middle Way, which he likened to the successful playing of the lute, the strings being not too taut, not too loose, but with just the right amount of pressure. We all need to seek a way to bring forth such balance in our own lives.

I deeply believe that it is vital to our spiritual practice that we become spiritually disciplined. Without spiritual discipline we are never going to wake up or advance on our soul's journey through this life. But our discipline must be wedded to joy, and we must find pleasure in the myriad wonders that this life offers.

I smile when I recall taking Buddhist friends, Tibetan and American, to the airport. A young monk asked the American Buddhist if he could wheel her carry-on through the airport, because it was maroon and better matched his robes than his own tan one. We all laughed, the woman complied, and the monk was color coordinated. He may have given up much of this world's offerings, but within him remained an artistic sense of color—balance.

For every ascetic I have known, I have known legends of overindulgent, spoiled consumers who live their lives as "hungry ghosts," never getting enough. The truth is that we can never fill ourselves up sufficiently with things to ever feel satisfied. There is no amount of beautiful stuff that can ever fill the empty soul and make us whole, loved and liberated.

It isn't that we can't enjoy the finer things in life, we just need to know they are not our life. Those practicing Middle Way know this. They can take in what is offered and available without being consumed by it. Their eyes discern beauty, even from the mundane. Their ears discern harmony from discordant notes. Their taste discerns pleasure from bland food. Their noses discern subtle notes of pleasant fragrance from the rancid.

We would have to be a bit off to choose the mundane, discordant, foul and putrid to believe these will lead to spiritual awakening. So we choose the pleasant and do not allow it to possess us. When we don't get what we would prefer, we don't allow ourselves to become unbalanced and miserable—adding to our own suffering. We see it for what it is, and we are able to remain detached and move on.

A good example and a recurring theme in my life is around eating and my food preferences. For most of my life I have not eaten meat. It was not something I forced upon myself. It was not a "should." One weekend meat simply gave me up. As a young child, I realized the steak, hot dog, pork chop and chicken thigh came from the body of an animal. I can still remember being shocked and thinking that it was so odd and gross that my mother and father, who were excellent cooks, were serving me meat and I was eating it. Being a dutiful child, I continued to eat meat to please my parents and others, unlike my friend Roger, who at age four told his mother he no longer wanted to eat any meat. She was aware enough to comply, and he has never had meat since.

So I don't eat meat. Many people do not really understand what that means. I love the scene from *My Big Fat Greek Wedding* where the heroine is introducing her fiancé to her aunt and mentions that for their forthcoming dinner together he does not eat meat. "What do you mean he don't eat meat? No meat?" She is so puzzled, and then the light dawns, as she cries out, "Good! I'll make lamb!" That line still makes me laugh.

There have been many a dinner party, a gathering where I have had to eat only the rice and peas and maybe an egg, and it is truly okay for me. I prefer more than that, but if that's what needs to be for me to remain true to my choice, then so be it. I realize that, since I am the one who has chosen to eat differently, I am more than willing to adapt to any situation.

An important and recurring theme in my life is balance. So many times this important lesson is driven home to me, and the irony of it is that often it is very humorous.

David and I went to France to celebrate my birthday. In Paris for five days, we stayed in a luxurious hotel providing every imaginable creature comfort down to the walls of our suite being padded and covered with soft peach silk. One could fall asleep in luxury just by leaning again the wall. It was a pleasure to the senses. By contrast, we next spent a week in a concrete, windowless cell at Thich Nhat Hanh's monastery, Plum Village. It was devoid of creature comforts but ripe with the purity of deep and engaged spiritual practices.

- Padded silk to concrete walls—balance.
- Lavish meals to organic, simple fare—balance.
- Late nights walking down the Champs-Élysée to 4 A.M. bell in the meditation hall—balance.
- Walking the halls of the Louvre to sitting in rapt attention to Thich Nhat Hanh's teachings—balance.

The strings of the lute of my life are not too lax, not too tight. There is a balance between the two—the Middle Way.

When we take the Middle Way we still have preferences, but we are not driven by them. We have sought for and found the balance. I have long thought that one of the most beautiful songs to come out of the seventies was from The Moody Blues, "The Balance." The lyrics, to paraphrase, are: Just open your eyes, just open your mind, and open your heart, and realize the way it's always been.

The Buddha realized the self-destructiveness of totally denying our desires, and the ultimate unhappiness of succumbing to all of them. Thus was born the concept of the Middle Way—having a balance that was not too rigid, not too slack, just like the strings of the lute.

To practice achieving the Middle Way in one's own life, first there must be the desire to live a balanced life. One must be awake enough to care about such things. It must be meaningful. Second, it is necessary to recognize when life has gotten out of balance and begin to bring in either more discipline or more pleasure. Seek to live as a conscious being, neither totally hedonistic nor totally ascetic.

A physician I met out of a personal medical need has over time become one of my nearest and dearest friends. She truly, sincerely cares about her patients. Not only does she tend to their medical needs in an extraordinary manner, she is brilliant in diagnostic work and the necessary follow-through. She also adds a spiritual dimension and prays for her very ill patients, sometimes even in the hospital setting. She is always willing to serve, to give a call to a medical colleague across the country to admit and attend to an unknown patient.

She is awesome in so many ways, but her life is not in balance. The scales are tipped way to one side with medical responsibilities, caring for her family, often flying around the country for speaking engagements. Sixteen- to twenty-hour days are all too commonplace, leaving her no time and little energy. We discuss how overwhelming her schedule is, and she says she'll do less, but it has not yet happened.

For many, perhaps especially career women, the demands of career and family leave very little time for self. Yet it is absolutely necessary to make sure there is time for meditation, prayer, entertainment, doing nothing, exercise, gardening, having lunch with a friend.

One way to begin to bring a bit of balance into your life is to look at your calendar or day planner with a discerning eye and clear one entire day each week. "Impossible!" the workaholic exclaims. Okay. Then revisit your calendar and eliminate just one appointment—a breakfast or lunch meeting, an after-school activity, a volunteer task—each day. It is not only possible but imperative to do so if you are to live a balanced life.

Do something just for yourself that will nurture your inner being at least twice a week. I do Pilates and take French lessons, both of which I love. They are just for me and not for anyone else in my life. Ask yourself what would bring you balance and pleasure. Is it hikes in the woods, watching a sporting event, participating in a sport, taking a painting class, taking a cooking class, learning to play chess, swimming? Find an activity you can greatly enjoy, one that will also clear your mind and calendar. Your life will be better for it.

Think of those you know personally who seem to have chosen the Middle Way. What do you see in them that you could begin to emulate? Balance can begin with acts as simple as turning off the computer or TV and taking a walk in nature, reading inspirational material or meditating for thirty minutes.

The Middle Way is not about never going to the movies or a club or shopping. It is about not making these things your life, the object of your existence. The Middle Way is also about remaining centered and spiritually poised when life is going your way and when it is not. The Middle Way is choosing peace in all circumstances. It is choosing love over the need to be right.

In our world fraught with violence and conflict, it is knowing there is *always* a Divine way out of the madness. The Middle Way is having the desire to find it.

Human compassion does not come from religious text.
Human compassion is in our blood.

—THE DALAI LAMA

The Four Immeasurables

I AM FILLED with love, compassion, joy and equanimity for the depth of meaning found in the Dalai Lama's simple words above.

Again and again my soul is endlessly drawn to the Four Immeasurables—Love, Compassion, Joy and Equanimity. Their depth and simplicity bring such comfort to me at times when comfort is needed. They bring such clarity of understanding when clarity is needed. They bring abiding insight into our ultimate nature when insight is sought.

It is profoundly meaningful that these four—Love, Compassion, Joy, Equanimity—are called Immeasurable because their magnitude is so enormous it cannot be measured. Just as the vastness of space cannot be measured, so, too, is it impossible ever to be able to measure the depth and breadth of influence of the Immeasurables. To master these four would truly be the accomplishment of a great being.

Students of Brahma went to the Buddha and asked, "What must we do to become like you?" The Buddha replied: "Daily practice the Four Immeasurables." By practicing them daily, you add to your happiness and the happiness of all those around you.

As we practice Love, Compassion, Joy and Equanimity, our hearts are healed. They soften and become open to all people and animals and to the environment and nature as a whole, seeing all as precious treasures to be highly valued. In faithfully practicing these four, all the madness and nonsense that has kept us separated from ourselves and others begins to be healed. The chasm begins to narrow. Light enters the shadowy places in consciousness and begins to bring forth profound healings on every level.

The Buddha said that the Four Immeasurables are the very nature of an enlightened person. In other words, as we advance on our journey of awakening, these are the very qualities that define who we are and what we are becoming.

LOVE

There are thousands of books on love, I myself having written a popular one, *A Course in Love.*

Love is immeasurable and so difficult to communicate through the written word. It is not sentimentality. It is not a commodity. If it's here today and gone tomorrow, it was never love. Love is at the very core of our being. When everything else is stripped away, true love remains. It is our essential core. We do not have to seek to become loving, but rather we must remove all the obstacles and obscurations to love's presence within us. This means systematically eliminating all judgments and all separating thoughts.

Consider the absolutely most loving person you know and observe his or her behavior. Ask yourself: How could I be more like that? How could I be more kind, thoughtful and loving?

Considering who I would pick is difficult, because my life has been blessed by so very many loving people—from my parents, who truly loved me, to my dear husband, to my precious friends with whom I share a soul-bond and walk a spiritual path. Instead of telling you about only one, I'll share what they all have in common, for they are all noble beings who personify love. Here are four characteristics:

1. In order to be an extraordinary loving person, the tantamount requirement is to love yourself. A self-effacing or self-loathing individual does poorly when it comes to loving others.

2. Loving people are all verbal. There is none of, "Oh, she knows I love her. I don't have to say it." Yes, we do need to say it and say it often. Be generous with your praise and acknowledgments. It is so important to simply *see* another person and tell her what you see.

3. A loving person is generous. Tightwads need not apply. One who truly loves has learned he lives in an abundant Universe and can afford to be generous.

4. A truly loving person has learned to care for and cherish others as much as self.

There are even more characteristics, but practicing these key ones will get you moving in a wonderful direction.

Practice being loving, doing loving acts for others you know—family, friends, colleagues, and for those you don't know. Engage in acts of loving-kindness throughout your day. Your heart will soften. You will become more accessible to others, and others will become more accessible to you. Practice truly listening to others. Practice truly seeing them. Catch others doing something grand and praise them.

COMPASSION

For many compassion takes years of practice. One beneficial way to practice is to engage in the technique of exchanging yourself for others. Depending on how difficult you consider the other person to be, you might find it more helpful to start to use this attribute with those whom you already love and who you know already love you.

To do this, visualize the other person. Pick a loved one who is experiencing a minor upset. See her in her current state, and imagine you can go directly into her and begin to feel what she is feeling. Remain very centered and continue to plug in on a soul/cellular level until a shift begins to take place within you. Breathe through her pain and discomfort until you feel a degree of release. Enfold her in light and love. Ask that she be protected by angels, dakinis, bodhisattvas or whatever protective image works for you. Then come out of the meditation through deep breathing and feel the clarity and freedom.

What I have learned in life about compassion is that we cannot know what we do not know. What that means is that we cannot truly understand something until we have personally experienced it. When we have suffered in a particular way, then we can have true compassion for others in similar circumstances. Such experiences afford us true compassion.

Compassion comes with spiritual maturity. When we have experienced much in life—sorrows and suffering, heartache and loss—we are seasoned to become either bitter or compassionate. The spiritual person chooses compassion. To be compassionate our hearts must truly be wide open. There can be no barriers or walls of protection. Then we can begin to experience the joys and triumphs.

JOY

When I think of His Holiness the Dalai Lama, I think of the most joyous person imaginable. To hear him laugh, to see his face light up with delight fills an auditorium with joy. He has not allowed the adversities and tragedies of his life and people to rob him of his immeasurable quality of unabashed joy and compassion that is in his blood.

Joy bubbles out of him like a sparkling fountain. Does he have the corner on how one can have a happy life? No, but for his seventy years he has from childhood practiced the Four Immeasurables. So, too, must we practice removing that which would keep joy a faint hope. We must see all the good, the blessing, the beneficial that is contained within an experience. Find what brings you joy and cultivate it more into your life.

Our two little Yorkshire terriers and our adopted-from-Hawaii kitty bring us great joy every day. They are just being themselves, but my husband, David, and I observe them through eyes of joy. So we attend to them lovingly. We are forever noticing their cute antics and poses and relish in what joy they have added to our lives.

The Dalai Lama speaks frequently about all people, all sentient beings, desiring happiness. He regularly emphasizes the importance of being happy and having a happy life, happiness and joy being one. How important has joy been in your life? What would it mean to you to have more joy and happiness? What would you have to give up to have more joy in your life? Do not quickly dismiss this important question. What stories would you have to cease from telling; what behaviors, beliefs and attitudes would have to be released?

I coached a friend whose life record seemed permanently stuck on the "they did me wrong" song. After years of hearing ancient and new versions of the same old story, out of utter frustration I said, "I've heard enough. Your life is never going to change until you change and divorce yourself from this unhealthy life-robbing situation." What I have always known and continue to know about this young man is that he will have his life-changing breakthrough. For now he still has more work to do to learn how to love himself enough to no longer tolerate in the future the abuses of the past.

Abe Lincoln said, ". . . most people are about as happy as they've made up their minds to be." Choose joy and you are choosing happiness for yourself and others. This is a truly blessed Immeasurable.

EQUANIMITY

Patrul Rinpoche teaches in *Words of My Perfect Teacher* that the Immeasurable he prefers to explore first is equanimity, which he refers to as impartiality, ". . . having an even-minded attitude towards all beings, free of attachment to those close to us and aversion for those who are distant."

The teachings on equanimity are very profound, and it takes at least an awakening mind to comprehend that all human beings hold equal value—not for their persona and accomplishments, but because, when all the layers of self are peeled away, what remains is the true spiritual essence, the Divine Nature which is all the same. It is one. No matter how glorious or how unskilled an individual's actions may seem, no matter what they are doing with their lives, beneath it all there lies a oneness. This is what we are called upon as noble beings to look upon.

When we can know this and see this, then we have spiritual sight. We are experiencing equanimity. When we can care as deeply for the sinner as we do for the saint, then it can be said that we are grasping equanimity. When we can embrace all with love, compassion and joy, then we are awakening to equanimity.

When attending the teachings of the Dalai Lama in Pasadena, California, I experienced as always a life-affirming and inspiring few days of sitting with pure holiness in the presence of an enlightened one.

One afternoon at the lunch break I exited the auditorium with the other 2,400 attendees and received a startling greeting of enormous contrast. Just beyond the boundaries of the convention center were about a dozen enraged men with bullhorns and nasty placards screeching at the Buddhist assemblage. They hurled insults at the monks and nuns in robes and at all the rest of us "stupid, stupid Americans."

I was taken aback and startled by their venomous rage, a glaring contrast to the peace and love in which I had just been swimming. Later I would see that those angry men were the perfect teachers assisting me to learn about equanimity along with the other three Immeasurables. I had to do much praying, forgiveness work and meditation to see this, but with practice the insights came. Then I could begin to see them as fearful of the unknown, just as in the past I had been fearful of the unknowns in my life.

These men were fearful of Tibetan Buddhist teachings and their leader, because their teachings told them there was only one holy man, and he lived thousands of years ago. They were fearful of the Buddhist teachings because they were unknown and not Christian. I must say that I saw and experienced a lot more "Christianity" inside the auditorium than out.

One Tibetan monk was busily snapping the whole scene on his camera. He got close-up shots of the men's contorted faces hurling insults at him—all the while being calm yet inquisitive, and taking none of it personally as he clicked away.

From earlier teachings of the Dalai Lama I remember him frequently saying that no one behaves so unskillfully unless he is deeply hurting and unhappy. Therefore we must have compassion. In all circumstances life calls on us to practice the Four Immeasurables—Love, Compassion, Joy and Equanimity.

The purpose of life is to be happy.

—HIS HOLINESS THE DALAI LAMA

A PATH TO HAPPINESS

A T AN OUTDOOR VENUE called Shoreline, near San Jose, His Holiness the Dalai Lama talked at length and stressed this point on happiness.

In our spiritual life we should never develop contentment—for our physical life, yes, but not for our spiritual life. One of my congregants once said to me, "I am finally ready to get off the road of least resistance and onto the 'road less traveled.'" To experience a genuine spiritual life we must be willing to travel the unfamiliar byways of the spiritual journey. We also must realize it is never-ending and come to peace with that fact.

To me one of the more appealing aspects of Buddhism is that the paths have been explored and developed and utilized by hundreds of thousands of monks and nuns over the past 2,600 years. They have spent lifetimes solely dedicated to their spiritual practice. And we in the twenty-first century can benefit from that. What has evolved are systematic formulas and practices that, when engaged correctly and meticulously, produce valuable results. One can take these teachings and superimpose these ageless methods and timeless ideas onto one's own soul exploration.

In our physical life it is good to become content with what is. This does not mean there is not room for improvement. But to advance without angst, to be content with who you are, where you are, what you have, with the circumstances of life, to cease from the painful desire to accumulate more and more, brings peace.

On the other hand, *never* be content with your spiritual life, because there is always more to learn and grow and deepen and become. Each awakening opens a door to a new room in consciousness where we learn to grow and become more. In turn, this leads to the next "aha," and we once again expand. The process is unending. We never arrive.

I first learned this teaching when I was in training for the ministry. It was not a welcomed teaching. The very idea of it felt exhausting because of the constant demands upon my soul and reevaluating thoughts and beliefs previously held as dear or as the truth. And through the years it has proven to be so. A friend of mine posed, "So is it that we *never* graduate?" This says it well. There is no sitting back and resting on our spiritual laurels if we are on a genuine path. No, we NEVER graduate.

We may know a lot, but it is the constant journey of awakening and going deeper that continues to fulfill us. As Jesus said, "The birds have their nests, and the foxes have their dens, but the son of man has nowhere to rest his head." You are "the son of man," and the truth of your being is that there is nowhere to go to get away from the spiritual work. We, unlike the animals, cannot escape to nest or den. Our journey is ongoing. And with each advance comes keener insights and greater awakenings and greater joy.

In this process of never being done, the Buddhists offer one of their wonderful, ancient formulas. To whatever is going on, we need to ask, "Is this beneficial?" "Is this harmful?" Then you focus one at a time on the five filters through which we can finely sift our thoughts and beliefs. These are referred to as the "five aggregates":

- Form
- Feeling
- Perceptions

- Mental formations
- Consciousness.

These five contain the whole of existence when we utilize them correctly. We are going to look at each, asking if we are experiencing each as harmful or beneficial.

THE FIVE AGGREGATES

Form:
This is our physical world, our body, things. Form does not endure.

Pause and gaze at your hand. Your hand is form, and your hand is not going to last forever. How am I treating my body, beneficially or harmfully? Is any particular possession of mine beneficial or harmful? Am I treating the environment beneficially or harmfully?

We ascribe to anything and everything all the meaning it has for us. Nothing in this world has an absolute and eternal meaning. We are constantly making the meaning up. Think of a chair. This chair has no meaning to me. Does an expensive chair have more meaning than an inexpensive chair? Are my thoughts about the chair beneficial or harmful? Someone spills coffee with cream on your expensive chair. Are your thoughts beneficial or harmful? Most likely they are harmful. This actually happened at our home shortly after I first wrote these words! All things considered, I was very pleased at my internal and external response.

Where we get "messed up" (using my vernacular to interpret the Buddhist concepts) is that we experience "mental sinking." That is, we think the chair will make us happy. As a matter of fact, we think our happiness depends upon that chair.

Form is anything we can touch. We need to always ask, "Is my attraction to this thing really attachment in disguise?" "Is it beneficial or harmful?" "Does my happiness depend upon that object?"

Feelings:

Let us say you are feeling happy, joyous, satisfied, compassionate. Is this a beneficial or harmful feeling? Obviously these are beneficial feelings. But if we are feeling separate, agitated and angry bordering on hatred, then we must be aware that these are harmful feelings. And they are harmful not just to us mentally and physically, but to everyone around us, to our environment. To express harmful feelings such as these by sending out this harmful energy is really an act of selfishness.

The Buddhists say that such feelings poison the blood. How interesting it is, in light of our present-day knowledge, just how harmful such negative states of mind can be to one's physical well-being, just how disease-producing this can be.

A great truth is that we have no neutral feelings. We always have feelings about the occurrences of life. They may be masked or denied or welcomed or fully expressed, but we always have them, and they are not neutral.

Perceptions:

Traveling the path we quickly begin to realize that our perceptions are just that—ours. One individual's perception is not more valuable than another's. Each of us perceives in our own, unique fashion. We practice by asking with each perception we hold, "Am I sure?" Am I sure that how I am seeing this situation is accurate? You can use "Am I sure?" as an inner filter.

"Am I sure?" always reminds me of couples I have counseled through the years. Often one or both of the parties is "sure" of the other's intention and assigns all manner of meaning to occurrences that, of themselves, are quite meaningless. Many resist accepting a situation that is not really factual but only one's own perception.

The ancient Buddhist text called *The Diamond Sutra* teaches, "Where there is perception there is deception." For me that teaching is extraordinary. Where there is perception there is deception. Perception-deception: pretty simple if we would only get it!

Mental formations:

These are our seed thoughts, our very core thoughts in the subconscious mind. They can be positive or negative.

These can be of love, kindness, generosity, equanimity, compassion, forgiveness, inclusiveness, or they can be focused on separation, grievance, anger, hatred, envy, jealousy, being the victim. What we do is water these seed thoughts. Perhaps we use a little watering can, or maybe we turn on a fireman's hose. We must ask, "Is this beneficial or harmful?" Is it beneficial or harmful to have this thought about this person relative to this experience?

Consciousness:

This is our individual thumbprint in the universe, and the Buddhist view of consciousness is exactly the same as the metaphysical view. It is the sum total of our being; it is who we are. Consciousness is our soul's DNA. It is always expanding or contracting. We must always be aware what seeds in our consciousness are being watered by ourselves or others.

This fifth aggregate contains the other four aggregates. Where our consciousness goes, our lives will follow. Following this discipline, I do not watch negative entertainment. I do not read negative or violent material. I am most mindful of what seeds of consciousness I am watering. I am always asking, "Is this beneficial or harmful?"

I broke my own "entertainment code" while going through a very consuming difficulty. I was praying constantly for a right outcome, and in spite of what was occurring, I was able to avoid "mental sinking" and remain quite centered. Then for "entertainment" I watched an extremely violent and disturbingly haunting Academy Award–winning movie.

The content of that film polluted the delicate balance that had been maintained in my consciousness in the midst of conflict. What immediately followed was a restless night filled with graphic images of horror occupying my brain. Also, I developed galloping worry about the current situation. My peace was displaced for about twelve hours, and it took a great deal of prayer, cleansing meditation and affirming to center myself once again. What a lessons on top of a lesson it was.

From our past thoughts comes our present state of mind. From our present thoughts will come our future state of mind. Our life is the creation of our minds.

If we speak or act with an impure mind, suffering will follow—as surely as the chariot follows the animal that draws it.

If we speak or act with a pure mind, joy will follow—as surely as the shadow follows the person who casts it.

Some people look at others and think: That person insulted me; that person upset me; that person defeated me; that person cheated me. Their minds are never free from hate. Those who do not think such thoughts are free from hate.

Hate is never appeased by hate; it is appeased by love. This is an eternal law.

—*THE DHAMMAPADA*

THREE FILTERS OF CONSCIOUSNESS

There are three filters to put over the lenses of the Five Aggregates to assist us in seeing clearly. They are:

1. Insight. Let me see insightfully.
2. Correct. Let me see correctly. Let my perceptions be correct.
3. Repeat. Let me see each form in the moment, not how it has been in the past or how it might be in the future, but right now. We constantly have to repeat our spiritual practice, engaging in this path repeatedly to grow. Early on my spiritual journey I learned this phrase: "Repetition, repetition, repetition." We re-

peat a spiritual truth long enough, and it becomes a part of our store consciousness.

An example of applying the three filters of consciousness took place while I was attending His Holiness the Dalai Lama's teachings in Los Angeles. I found that there were always plenty of parking spaces available in the sponsors' lot. Where oh where were the majority of the event's sponsors? Nowhere to be seen. Rows of empty seats and an abundance of parking spaces in the sponsors' lot. The early days of teaching were always filled with intense and often very challenging-to-understand material. Often the Tibetan teaching method is not very engaging to the Western mind.

On the last day, the day a blessing was to be bestowed on the attendees, the previously partially empty parking lot was not only full to capacity but overflowing. Every possible space had a car squeezed into it. It was obvious that many more people had shown up for the sweetness of the blessing over the intensity of the teaching in a hot, dark, smelly, uncomfortable arena.

For me it was an interesting observation on human nature and the desire for so many to take the easy road rather than the "road less traveled." To advance spiritually always means to choose the demanding path. How many are actually willing to do so? Sometimes it appears that the answer is not that many. Let me see insightfully. Let me see correctly. Let me see into the now.

One step on the demanding path is to live peacefully. When I was young, I thought America was a peace-loving country. Then came Vietnam, then the first Gulf War, then the attack on Iraq. As a nation when we are challenged, or think we are, any guise of peace evaporates, and we attack. We responded to 9/11 with anger and pride—attack—which unfortunately seems to be the American nature.

The true warrior of the enlightened mind seeks peace in every instance. The bodhisattva mind has no anger or pride or need to attack. One seeking the path to enlightenment always chooses peace. That is why I study with the Dalai Lama. He always chooses peace. A noble being seeks to experience unity and harmony, both in life's great moments and in ordinary daily life, as well as in life's tragic moments.

As we journey toward living an awakened life, it is only natural and appropriate that we be happy. Living a so-called spiritual life and at the same time being a miserable and suffering martyr went out of style centuries ago.

When we are happy as an awake being, then our desire for all others is that they, too, experience happiness. It is here that we can know our innate oneness. It is here that any sense of separation begins to dissolve and the true essence of each individual can come forth. This awareness does not drop from the sky. It must be remembered. It must be realized in our hearts. Then we must practice. Then we must repeat those practices again and again. We all need to engage techniques and formulas that appeal to reason and lead to higher states of awareness. This is how we come to wake up, to be able to see through the veil, past the illusions and into the truth that lies in waiting within us all.

A path to happiness comes to us all as we mindfully journey on our path, committed to engaging these blessed teachings at all times under all circumstances. For this material to have any true meaning, it must be embraced intellectually, because it is reasonable, psychologically sound and simply makes sense. And then it must make two subsequent journeys. First, it must travel from the head to the heart. Here the heart is healed if healing is needed, and then the heart opens. Second, with an open heart one can experience life so much more fully.

I have found on my path, as my heart continues to open, I am deeply touched by the preciousness of life. I witness a tender exchange between a little girl and her daddy and I fill up with tears. On Veterans Day I read an article on the remaining World War I veterans, and I get choked up.

On November 11, several years back, David and I arrived in Paris and were walking toward the Arc de Triomphe unaware in that moment that it was Armistice Day, as Europeans call that day. When we arrived, to our amazement, thousands of people were ringing the monument, which was flying the French flag. We were moved to tears at the deep importance of this day for the French.

Another life-changing incident occurred when we were at Juno Beach in Normandy. Juno is the D-Day beach where our Canadian neighbors first landed. The enormity of the beaches and the memory of what occurred more than sixty years ago remains alive in me to this day. Upon arriving at the beach, my husband and I walked for a few minutes in opposite directions. While I was alone, an elderly French gentleman wearing a beret approached me and asked in French if I was an American. "*Oui, monsieur*," I replied. His clear, steel-gray eyes looked deeply into mine, and he simply said, "*Merci beaucoup, merci beaucoup.*" My heart burst open. Here he was thanking me! I wasn't even born and had nothing to do with D-Day and the liberation of the French, his liberation, but he was still deeply grateful. It was so astonishing and meaningful to me that I could not hold back the tears. (When I reread these words, I wept again.)

When our hearts are open, life in its true, loving expression can flow through us and from us. We feel beauty and pathos. We can exchange our sense of self with another. Rainbows and thunderstorms alike have danced in my heart, all because long ago I became committed to doing whatever it took to open my heart and keep it open.

To walk that glorious path to happiness, know it is safe and necessary to open your heart and clear your life of mental distractions, obscurations, and embrace your innate holiness.

The teaching of Tibetan Buddhism offers us in the West phenomenal techniques and processes that have been practiced for nearly 2,600 years. They offer us the unvarnished truth. They work. They have proven themselves to be beneficial through the ages. Now in our time this ancient wisdom is available to us. We can daily practice The Four Immeasurables— love, compassion, joy and equanimity. We can consistently engage the Five Aggregates—form, feelings, perceptions, mental formations and consciousness. These all help us to reap the benefit of oneness, knowing unity with our fellow travelers.

FIVE AGGREGATES EXERCISES

Practice each of the following exercises, one a week for five weeks:

Form

First, in meditation, as well as in an awakened state of outer awareness, look at your hand. Look deeply. What do you see? Very often I see my mother's hand when I look at my own. Ask yourself, What does this hand, face, leg, etc., mean to me?

Second, pick an object in your home that holds great importance for you. Look at it deeply. What do you see? If it were lost or stolen or destroyed in some way, how would you feel? Put it out of your sight for the week. Do you miss it? Realize it is just a "thing," and you have given it all the meaning you ascribe to it.

Feelings

For the next week, write down your feelings three times a day in your journal or, if you don't have one, a small notebook. Keep it simple. This needn't be complicated or complex. For example:

7 A.M.—Expectant, feeling of well-being.
2 P.M.—Centered, lighthearted.
10 P.M.—Pleased, sleepy.
   or
7 A.M.—Anxious, nervous.
2:00 P.M.—Stressed, burned out.
10:00 P.M.—Exhausted, anxious.

It should be easy to see which feelings are beneficial and which are harmful.

Perceptions

"Where there is perception, there is deception." This is a very helpful yet simple exercise to do in the third week. Get a half-dozen note cards and write in bold lettering: **Am I sure?** Place them around your home, workplace, auto, in your wallet—wherever you will see them frequently.

Ask yourself frequently throughout each day, Am I sure my perception is correct? Am I sure he's really this way? Am I sure I must have this?

An attorney in my congregation asked herself this question as she was about to pass up the deal of the decade on a very expensive mink coat. Did she want the money in her retirement account, or did she want the mink, of which she already had several?

Am I sure I need this, want this, want to spend the money? Why do I need this, want this? What is this coat offering to me? Will it make me happy or beautiful?

Am I sure?

Mental Formations

In the fourth week work with the concept, Is this helpful? Do the exercise much like the preceding one. This time take note cards and write on each, *Is this beneficial or harmful?* Then post them where you spend your days, as in the previous week.

Is this thought, feeling, action, belief, attitude, judgment beneficial or harmful?

If you do this exercise with great honesty, you may be quite surprised. If your answer is harmful, you have your work cut out for you.

Consciousness

Remember that consciousness contains the previous four aggregates. A very helpful exercise is always to be mindful of what you call entertainment and what you allow to be programmed into your subconscious mind.

We all need to know what's going on in this world, but we do not need to be witness to all the horrors and atrocities happening around the globe. All four of my grandparents were immigrants, arriving in the United States ranging in age from toddlers to teens. They were never aware daily of the global horrors of their era. They didn't have the Internet, CNN, Fox, CNBC, etc., the constant media bombardment. Life was simple for them because of this.

THE THREE JEWELS

THE THREE JEWELS of Buddhism are considered jewels because of the preciousness and valued wisdom that is contained within them. They could be likened to the parable of the Pearl of Great Price from the Bible.

The teachings of life are incredibly demanding, pushing us against the wall. We must call upon everything we have ever known to receive true and deep teachings, not necessarily a "good" feeling. We so often want the goodies, the loaves and the fishes. We desire the treats without the strenuous years of arduous study, work and preparation.

We don't want the arduousness of the journey. We just want the blessing at the end. This is our ego nature at work. We are not interested in the demands of spiritual life. In the Three Jewels we are given three avenues to focus on in our spiritual life—the Buddha, the Dharma, the Sangha.

In Christian thought an equivalent three would be Christ consciousness or God, the spiritual teachings, and the spiritual community or church.

The Three Jewels are the place for us to go to take refuge. Refuge is a concept that we in the West do not generally entertain. It is a haven, a place of peace and safety for the mind, body and soul in order to deepen our spiritual practice. We do not seek refuge in the impermanent, for there we would be left directionless.

The concept of refuge was very prominent in ancient Hawaiian culture. On each island of the Hawaiian chain there was a place of safe haven called "the city of refuge." Here a warrior who was being pursued for whatever reason could go and seek refuge. Once inside, he or she would be safe and free from authorities. It was a sacred place that gave refuge to all who entered. In Buddhism refuge takes the form of the Three Jewels, rather than being a physical location.

When we fully understand the concept of refuge, we realize we need to take refuge daily, as the Buddhists teach. We all face challenges, those painful times when we are experiencing a great loss through illness or death or troubles at work or within the family, for example. At such times our souls, our psyches, need to find a place of solace, somewhere to go— be it physically or mentally—where we can rest and be renewed. A true place of refuge must be spiritually based, not worldly based. We cannot authentically say, "I take refuge in the refrigerator and the goodies therein," or "I take refuge in my expensive shoes." These worldly things may give temporary pleasure, but they cannot give refuge.

The First Jewel of Buddhism that offers us refuge is the Buddha, but not the historic Buddha. It is as the Buddha himself said on his deathbed, "Know that that means the Buddha in you." We all carry a divine nature within our spirits and souls. We could call it our true nature—the Buddha within, the Christ within.

A Western equivalent of this First Jewel is the Christ within you or the Spirit of God within you. It matters not what you call it. What matters is that you train yourself to immediately go there and no longer go to a place of fear or angst. Take refuge in your true, divine nature.

Two highly respected physicians who are close friends of ours went through nearly identical circumstances. Both lost honored positions through no fault of their own, due to a new chief of staff bringing in his cronies. With no compunction he let a highly regarded surgeon and researcher be dismissed.

They were equally stunned and shaken with disbelief. The impermanence of life and their positions arose to meet them both. Thankfully both are deeply spiritual and can take refuge in their spiritual practices and community. So they were able to take refuge in the first, second and third jewels.

We never know in life. Life throws us a curveball, and we can be caught very unaware. It is crucial that the Three Jewels be engaged in our lives to keep us in balance.

The Second Jewel, the Dharma, equates with spiritual teachings. The Dharma is the whole body of the teachings of Buddhism. The sacred texts, the ancient teachings passed down through oral tradition as well as passed down from teacher to individual student, all together constitute the Dharma.

We take solace in troubling times of our lives in the Dharma with our spiritual belief system based upon the teachings on a daily basis. If you do not find comfort and inspiration in your current faith, then perhaps it is time to closely examine why you are staying engaged in a system that does not nurture you. We must be able, in absolutely every set of life's circumstances, to find solace in our spiritual practices and teachings.

For those of us in Western spiritual thought—be it Christian or Jewish—the Dharma (perhaps the Bible, *A Course in Miracles* or other spiritual texts) must be meaningful. If it is not, we owe it to ourselves to seek a path that holds real value for our souls.

Although I would not have used such languaging at the time, when years ago I began to explore outside the borders of my Catholicism, I was seeking a more meaningful dharma. Dogma and dharma are vastly different. Dogma contains the dictates of religion, whereas Dharma is the body of spiritual teachings. Dogma is often cloaked in guilt. Dharma never is. Only the very fear-filled can find any kind of refuge in dogma.

It is the eternal spiritual teachings that bring us understanding. This leads to knowing, which in turn brings comfort to our souls when they are weary and in need of a resting place. It is helpful to question our current religious belief system to see if it is meeting the criteria of dharma.

Ask yourself, "Is my belief system meaningful, comforting, true and supporting my spiritual growth?"

Buddhist teachings are ageless and eternal. They are the truth. They are certainly not the only thought system that presents the truth, but they do embody the truth. Most of us have been in situations of disagreement with another where one person says something like this: "You have your truth and I have mine. They are just different, so let's simply agree to disagree." This conversation is not about the truth. It is about opinions, judgments. It would be more accurate to say, "You have your opinion and I have mine," or "You have your judgment and I have mine."

The truth is not an opinion. It is not a judgment. It is not a variable. It cannot be altered or divided. It simply is. It is as true today as it was two thousand years ago or ten thousand years ago. Truth is eternal. I explain in depth the working of truth principles, what they are, how to recognize them and come to live by them in my book *A Course in Life.*

The Third Jewel is the Sangha, the spiritual community where we can seek refuge when needed, where we can be a part of a collective consciousness that supports one another, where we can be with like-minded people. I have long believed strongly that everyone needs a spiritual community. The Buddha taught this, and I am happy to have him back me up!

The Sangha is your church, your temple. It is made up of the clergy, women, men and children of the particular community. The Sangha is those of harmonious minds coming together in order to join as a group in spiritual practice, spiritual discipline and worship.

What I have called a "cowboy mentality" my husband, David, calls an "American mentality." *I can go it alone. I don't need any help. I don't need anybody. Yep, it's just me against the world.* It's that individuality of expression usually coming from the ego that I don't believe is helpful or serves us well.

In contrast, the spiritual teaching is that we need to be with like-minded people with whom we are attuned. We need a spiritual community that we call our home, our church, our temple, our sangha. No matter how strong we are in our individual spiritual practice, it can still be difficult for us to continue without the support and camaraderie of the group. It is a basic need to be with like-minded people—to go to, to love, to practice, to be connected.

While at Plum Village in Dordogne, France, on a retreat with Thich Nhat Hanh, David and I were discovering ways to deepen our practice. At this particular time we were the only "short-timers" at the retreat. None of the others, who were there for months or years, knew who we were or what we did back in America.

There was a young German woman in residence who was always telling me what to do, from peeling an apple to how to wash pots and pans. When her "helpful" suggestions were put forth, I would slowly breathe in and out, smile and follow orders. It was a great exercise in keeping my ego in check, since I pride myself on knowing my way around a kitchen quite well and on being a gourmet cook. One morning during breakfast preparation, she inquired as to what I did professionally back in the States. At this point no one knew, so I said I was an author. She, who had just been carefully telling me how to peel an apple, looked at me quizzically. Then she asked if I had a sangha. After a few moments' pause, I said, "Yes, I do, and I'm the leader of the sangha." Then I added that I was the minister of a nondenominational church. Her whole attitude toward me changed immediately, which was exactly what I did not want. All in all it was quite cosmically funny. All of a sudden, after about five days of being ordered about, my status was elevated.

Through the years I have known ministers and congregants who have pulled away, wanting nothing more to do with group energy and dynamics. I have never observed this to be beneficial for those individuals. Often afterward they have met with dire consequences in their lives.

To develop wisdom we need to be aware of the pitfalls that can befall one who pulls away from the support of their spiritual family, their sangha. Says the Dalai Lama: "The Dharma is a mirror to look deeply into your own life at what is being reflected. Whatever is being reflected in your life, there is your teacher to look deeply and correct what is in error in body, speech and mind." He continued, "We must fully integrate these teachings into our own lives."

We must move beyond the intellectual knowing of these teachings until they become our experience. Ask, "What relevance does this have to my life today?" It is relevant if it brings what we know in the intellect of our minds into our hearts, into a specific situation, into our lives.

While with Thich Nhat Hanh, who was speaking on the Three Jewels, he said, "These are not just notions. These are your life." We must learn to fully integrate these teachings into our own lives—integrating knowledge and the practice of that knowledge with compassion, and to always have compassion with ourselves and where we are on the path and for others who may not be where we are on the path. You may be making tremendous strides, while many around you are still living as toddlers. This is such an important reminder when we are about to grow impatient with others because they are not where we are on the path.

We can learn to integrate all three of these into our hearts. They become the energy out of which we live our lives. The Buddha said at the conclusion of his life:

"Dear friends—humans, gods, Brahmans, monastics, and marashs—as witnesses, I tell you that if I have not experienced directly all that I have told you, I would not proclaim that I am an enlightened person, free from suffering. Because I myself have identified suffering, understood suffering, understood the cause of suffering, removed the cause of suffering, confirmed the existence of well-being, gone to the end of the path, and realized total realization."

Thich Nhat Hanh responded to that quote by saying, "At that moment the earth shook, and the voices of the gods, humans and other living beings throughout the cosmos said, 'On the planet earth an enlightened person had been born and put into motion the wheel of the dharma, the way of understanding and love.'"

So it was that the wheel of the dharma turned with the Buddha's awakening. The wheel of the dharma turned with Jesus Christ's resurrection. With these two acts of awakening and enlightenment came greater opportunity for us all. We must engage these Three Jewels and embrace the opportunities that have been given us.

Here is a spiritual practice that we can engage in daily while holding and counting mala beads or counting with your fingers (much more tedious). Chant at each count, "I seek refuge in the Buddha, Dharma and Sangha." A Christian version would be, "I seek refuge in the Christ, the teaching and my spiritual community." Take a deep, easy breath after each conscious repetition, and after a few dozen you will feel yourself calming down and centering. Do this on each of the 108 beads daily, and in time you will experience an increasingly permanent calming and relaxing of your mind.

I had a personal opportunity to directly apply this technique and exercise when I was leaving a Sogyal Rinpoche retreat in Northern California. The area was totally unknown to me as I drove my rental car on the switchback roads alone. I was practicing breathing and remained centered, even in the frightening driving conditions. It occurred to me to call my mother to check on her and to share some of my experiences of the extended retreat.

An unfamiliar male voice answered my call. It was a little disconcerting, until I realized it was a male relative who would seldom visit. It was also unsettling because he was always highly critical of my spiritual study and interest in Buddhism. And here we were, on the telephone with each other just after I had left a Buddhist retreat! My relative's sardonic attitude had not changed but, thank God and the Buddha, my response had. I remained centered and calm, not responding to any of the worn-out jabs pointed in my direction.

Shortly after ending the conversation I came upon a scenic overlook. I pulled off and drank in the beautiful vista. Then I began to pray on each of the 108 beads of my mala bracelet: "I seek refuge in the Buddha, the

Dharma and the Sangha." I did four complete sets, which took about twenty minutes, and I subsequently felt totally at peace. Applying the refuge exercise immediately proved to be most beneficial, resulting in warm feelings for my relative instead of hurt, fearful ones.

With a clearing of the mind comes peace and seeking refuge where it truly can be found.

When things are desperate, there is no need to pretend
that everything is beautiful.

—HIS HOLINESS THE DALAI LAMA

SPIRITUAL MEDICINE

A TEACHING BY His Holiness the Dalai Lama was sponsored by "The Land of the Medicine Buddha," a sangha in California located on eighty-five acres of magical, tranquil land adjacent to ten thousand acres of federal land. At the closing ceremonies for this beautiful teaching, a chorus of children of the sangha sang in precious, clear, little voices to the Dalai Lama:

How great it would be if all beings were free from suffering.

How great it would be when all beings were happy living without pain for all time to come.

The Dalai Lama leaned forward with his hand on his chin and cracked up! They were so cute, so adorable. The children continued to sing, and their chorus was:

Om, Madna, Padna, Hum.

The Dalai Lama started to chant the chorus along with the children, then the monks joined in, then the sixteen thousand in attendance joined in in a holy instant during which all sang:

Om, Madna, Padna, Hum.

Then the children continued: *I will help them to find this happiness.*

Then all: *Om, Madna, Padna, Hum.*

The children: *How great it will be if all beings were free, if we all loved everyone equally.*

All: *Om, Madna, Padna, Hum.*

I was moved, deeply moved, and my heart was filled. What the "Medicine Buddha" sangha is about is healing. And healing certainly was occurring in that space. Lama Zopa Rinpoche, who sponsored the Dalai Lama's visit, is a delightful presence and a radiant light from Santa Cruz. He said, "The Medicine Buddha is the manifestation of the healing energy of all enlightened beings. Symbolically coming together here in this one presence in our own lives, we can become one of the healed, enlightened beings."

One way to cure disease is through one's own mind, with meditation. Not only is this an effective method, but there are also no negative side effects. As well as healing, meditation promotes peace, calm and tranquillity in your heart. And the happiness you experience is transmitted to others, and thus you benefit them, as well.

This is the energy of the Medicine Buddha. It opens our minds and softens our hearts. We can think of it as "spiritual medicine" with no side effects. What a fabulous concept that we can all use: medicine for our souls.

Said the Dalai Lama, "Just as particular medication is not suitable for all people with a particular illness or ailment, one type of spiritual medication cannot be applied to every single person with an illness of the soul." An intense course of meditation would work for one, retreats for another, deep forgiveness for another. What is right and helpful for one may not be what is right for another because of the fact that our woundings are different and our needs for healing vary from person to person. We must find what spiritual medicine works for us.

There are many spiritual medications we can take, and they never have ill side effects. They all have positive side effects. For example:

If one had tremendous judgment and animosity toward another person's organizations or certain groups of people, the "medicine" would be forgiveness, love and compassion. These medicines, when practiced well, will help the individual achieve freedom from the suffering that such states of mind bring. Also, he can gain insight into his own nature and see how he is like that which he holds such a grievance against. When he discovers he has the same hopes and fears and dreams as the person or groups he judges, he can develop compassion rather than hatred for them. This is the kind of result that comes from consistent, faithful use of spiritual medicine.

Then, as the hatred, judgments and animosity begin to leave us and dissolve from our minds, they are replaced with understanding, thoughts of loving kindness, and compassion. We begin to see that individual as a spiritual sister, someone just like me. This assists us in our own healing and empowers us in healing others in need.

How does this precious teaching fit us today in our society and culture? How can I remember to use the spiritual medicines that are right for me? You will know by the results, or as Jesus said, "by the fruits." You will know they are right when your suffering is declining and your well-being is increasing. It is having a positive effect so that you begin to live up to your potential and begin to be a noble one. You are liberating your own soul.

Very often the Dalai Lama is intently attended to by an absolutely luminous being. And there he was at the Medicine Buddha teaching. This unassuming, humble monk has a translucent quality about him. He literally appears as if he is lit from within. He's onto something powerful. I love to open my heart and simply watch him as his glowing presence tenderly attends to His Holiness. It is taught that luminosity is the hallmark of an enlightened being.

As we work with spiritual medicine, it has to meet us where we are. Just remember that all spiritual medicines are not for all spiritual practitioners. This allows us to be more tolerant, more understanding of those in various religious traditions—those friends who think very differently than we do, those family members who think very differently than we do.

What they need for spiritual medicine is not the same as what you need for spiritual medicine.

Those of us who have left traditional religions often look back and realize that the spiritual medicine of those systems did not cure our ills for a very long time. We ask: Did my heart and soul begin to leave a long time ago? We decide: This isn't for me anymore, even though at one time it was and may still be for friends and relatives.

We need to always be mindful of the fact that, just because of where we may be today, in our zealousness we may want to convince our friends to embrace our new way. Please remember that the concept of conversion is one that appeals only to the unenlightened mind. In other words, do not attempt to convert your friends or relatives to your way of thinking and believing. I look at missionaries attempting to convert native peoples to their foreign religion, and I am deeply puzzled by this concept. What is the point? Is it beneficial?

My husband and I spend as much time as we can on the Hawaiian island of Molokai, the only island not invaded (for invasion it was) by missionaries. The damage that was done and the deep-seeded sorrow over loss of culture, language and religion is still palatable with the Hawaiian people today. This is all because Western missionaries believed it was their mission to bring Christianity to peoples that already were living for an aeon with deep spiritual practices on every level of their existence. The drive to covet propels some well-intended but misguided souls to this day, thinking their medicine is the Divine remedy for everyone who doesn't believe as they do, particularly native peoples.

YEARS AGO there was a very troubled young woman in my congregation who wrestled daily with deep feelings of rejection and abandonment that stemmed from her early childhood. Mary Sue was only six when her family moved from the United States to Japan, where her parents were about to begin a six-year stint as Protestant missionaries.

Her older siblings, who all moved to Japan, were immediately placed in a special English-speaking school for the children of missionaries. Mary Sue, being so much younger than her brothers and sisters, was sent off to another school for very young children to be boarded and "educated." Most of her education was in abandonment. Some years she was visited only twice by her mother and not at all by her father. The experience devastated her soul and self-esteem. For many years she has worked at filling the holes in her psyche. To this day her pain is still very real, as is her confusion and resentment.

This child lived in a foreign environment as a virtual orphan, and I dare say her misguided parents were busy trying to convert Japanese Zen Buddhists into Lutherans. It is simply staggering what some people consider valuable at the cost of losing their own children and family. As an adult, Mary Sue sought many forms of spiritual medicine, for she was wise enough to realize just how wounded she was.

After several years of therapy and after she was an adult, she attempted to speak to her parents about the devastating impact those six years in Japan had on her. Her parents simply did not want to hear it and would not listen. As Jesus said, they simply did not have the ears to hear.

After that, her spiritual medicine turned to engaging many forgiveness practices. It took many more years, but now she is much healed. She has lost a hundred pounds of "protective" weight, is working at what she loves, is acknowledged, appreciated and feeling good about herself. She learned how to heal her past and love herself.

In my opinion the entire notion of conversion comes from the missionaries' own self-doubt and questioning that has never been addressed. All their religious practices are projected outside the individual. While engaged in the acts of conversion, this doubt will never be addressed.

Spiritual medicine changes as we travel on our journey toward enlightenment. Many holy teachers remind us that a common factor in all great spiritual teachers is that they have endured great periods of hardship. We metaphysical types do not like to acknowledge the hardships of life. Don't we just wish this wasn't so? It's hard to perceive accurately through rose-colored glasses. If everything isn't fabulous, the sleeping metaphysician thinks, then you'd better not speak of it because what we focus on expands. What also expands, I believe, is our avoidance of some of the harsher experiences in life.

We need to accept and not be fearful of the fact that there are and will be times in life that are really tough. There are difficult times when we will be sick, when we or a loved one will suffer greatly, when someone we love will die, when we will be at the top of our game and then tumble. There are times when our world will be thrown into utter chaos. That happens. It is part of the journey. Life is impermanent.

When I heard the Dalai Lama say this, I pondered how true this had been in his life. As a young leader of his people at age twenty-one, he had to flee Tibet under cover. More than a million Tibetans have since been murdered by the Chinese communists. Thousands of Buddhist monasteries have been destroyed. He has personally known suffering deeply. The Dalai Lama has compassion for the perpetrators, but do not for a moment think he lives in a realm above it all. It has been most difficult for him. I have witnessed this precious man weep over the tragedies that have occurred, the sufferings he has endured and the ongoing sufferings of his people. But the tragedies do not define him. They have not, cannot, erode his true essence.

I thought of the extreme difficulties confronting Jesus, Gandhi, Martin Luther King, Thich Nhat Hanh. I thought of the suffering of those to whom I have ministered, know well and have journeyed with. Interestingly, even followers of Buddhism often want to avoid the reality of suffering and impermanence.

Does this sound familiar? We go through a period of hardship, and often we make ourselves at fault. Instead, we need to seek the appropriate spiritual medicine so our lives can be healed, and we can become an example, an inspiration, to others because we've gone through the fire. We've gone through our own process of alchemy and we've come out the other side a different person.

At the spiritual medicine teaching I attended, participants were given a 2-by-2½-inch 3-D image of the Buddha. It is called a tsa and can be held in one's hand during meditation. If I do not feel well or am experiencing an illness, it has its special place on my nightstand. This Medicine Buddha is a clear shade of blue, and just looking at it is comforting.

Let us remember the words of His Holiness the Dalai Lama: "When things are desperate, there is no need to pretend everything is beautiful." But let us also remember, there is a way out of our suffering.

*Those who recite many scriptures, but fail to practice their
teachings, are like a cowherd counting another's cows.
They do not share in the joys of spiritual life.*

—THE DHAMMAPADA, VERSE 19

THE FOUR FACTORS

I WAS TALKING to a seventy-five-year-old woman who, as she shampooed my hair at the beauty salon, was engaging me in conversation about Tibetan Buddhism. "I really want to know more about Buddhism," she said. So I regaled her with many of the Buddhist precepts for the next twenty-five minutes. She paid rapt attention. She was mesmerized and delighted.

After a while she said, "I really admire Tina Turner, Patti Labelle and Oprah. I figure if it's okay for them to study Buddhism, then its okay for me, too." I talked about the Four Noble Truths, the Eight-fold Path, reality, illusions, samsara and on and on. When I was about to leave, she thanked me and then said, "If I talked about any of this with my family, they would just say it was the devil. But I know better. I just know it's important that I study and learn more."

My judgment may be showing, but this kind of conservative Christian attitude is one of many that keeps us separate from one another in our world. The woman asked, "Is Buddhism a religion?" Buddhists would consider it a path, rather than a religion, as would congregants in Unity, my church, consider our faith a path, not a religion. The reason it is not a religion is that neither we nor the Buddhists have dogma and creeds you must believe. We both have very helpful and beneficial teachings that can lead one to awaken to one's true, luminous self.

The Four Factors, which we consider here, are the very nature of an enlightened person. They constitute a genuine spiritual practice. In a genuine spiritual practice we are called upon to engage our intellect, to use wisdom, to use our minds and never to revert to narrow thinking.

The First Factor is based on authentic scripture. For our spiritual practice to be genuine, it cannot be based on air. It must have a solid, provable base. Therefore the First Factor is based on scripture, not just any discourse, but authentic scripture.

In our Judeo-Christian thought, authentic scripture is the Bible, to which I would add the Gnostic Gospels. These, along with the books of the Dead Sea Scrolls, give us a broader base view of early Christian writing. They are believed by many to offer a more accurate telling of the tales of Jesus Christ, his life and his purpose. The First Factor found in the foundation of Buddhism is the *Dhammapada* and the ancient sutras, said to represent the words of the Buddha, such as the Diamond Sutra or the Heart Sutra.

These sutras offer very advanced teachings that are best studied with a qualified teacher. Here is one of my favorite passages from the Heart Sutra:

Form is emptiness and the very emptiness is form; emptiness does not differ from form. Form does not differ from emptiness; whatever is emptiness, that is form. The same is true of feelings, perceptions, impulses and consciousness. . . .

In emptiness there is no form nor feeling, nor perception, nor impulse, nor consciousness; no eye, ear, nose, tongue, body, mind; no forms, sounds, smells, taste, touchables, or objects of mind; . . .

A bodhisattva can overcome what can upset, and in the end he attains Nirvana.

The Heart Sutra is beautifully expressed in the movie *Little Buddha*, which my husband, David, and I have seen and enjoyed countless times. I highly recommend you watch it. Look for the short, round monk in an early scene talking with Bridget Fonda, who plays the young boy's mother. That is Sogyal Rinpoche.

The Second Factor in our spiritual checklist are the many authentic commentaries. Using our wisdom, we decide what is an authentic commentary, because there are endless opportunities to be duped. Jesus warned against "false prophets," and through the years I have encountered any number of them—often self-published, channeled or dogmatic books and teachers.

An authentic Buddhist commentary is Shantideva's works, or any work by highly respected sages and saints throughout history. For me, for the past thirty years, *A Course in Miracles* has been an authentic commentary. The works of Unity cofounders Charles and Myrtle Fillmore, along with Ernest Holmes of Religious Science, contain authentic commentaries.

An authentic commentary stands the test of time, and the reason this is so is because it contains the absolute, changeless truth. It teaches absolute reality rather than relative or conventional reality.

The Third Factor is to study with an authentic teacher. A true teacher demonstrates passion, clarity and commitment and walks his talk. Again, I have encountered many false prophets. If you are tuned in at all, your intuition will be communicating to you to stay away from slippery teachers. Here are the warning signs: a huge ego, attracting students through a charismatic, didactic personality, often using his sexuality as a lure, a controller who has all the answers—especially yours and is quite willing to tell you what to do.

A genuine teacher encourages her students to learn to go within and discover their own inner answers. A true teacher is spiritually humble, yet she knows who she is. She gathers her wisdom from years of study and practice and meditation. She demonstrates clarity, commitment, zeal and excitement for the teachings. And most important, she is manifesting what she is teaching.

I heard Sogyal Rinpoche say that it is hard to go home and meditate for an hour when you've been ranting at the office all day. When you look at a teacher, ask yourself if you want to emulate him. Do I aspire to be as he is?

When I was just out of college, I met for the first time a group of young Unity ministers while doing a biofeedback demonstration at Unity Village. I inwardly recognized that they had something I did not have, and I knew I wanted whatever that indefinable something was. I wanted to emulate the luminosity that they were manifesting. Today I want to emulate His Holiness the Dalai Lama, or Thich Nhat Hanh, or Sogyal Rinpoche or Jesus Christ.

An authentic teacher teaches not just with words but through the living of his life. As has been said by a number of great beings, including Gandhi, "My life is my message."

One message I have long taught is that everyone needs a teacher. The ego believes it has all the answers and can forgo having a teacher. The ego asks, What's the need? The wise one knows the best guardian at the ego's gate is an authentic teacher. Remember this, even the Dalai Lama has teachers whom he highly respects and with whom he consults.

A frequent common denominator I have witnessed with false teachers is that they dance with their sexual energy rather than commune with their inner divinity. Sexual energy can be very powerful and charismatic and alluring, but it is not of the Buddha nature, the Christ nature. Keep your eyes open, your feet on the ground and use your own inner guidance in choosing a teacher. But be mindful not to be duped.

A number of years ago I traveled to India, an arduous journey undertaken with two women friends, sisters on the path. They were going to visit their teacher, something they had done on several previous occasions. Intrigued, I went along to see if he would be my teacher, as well.

The conditions were very primitive, and we sat for hours in 110-degree heat in darshan (silently sitting and waiting for the teacher to arrive). After the fourth day of this, I realized I was not seeing an aura, that glowing color or light, emanating from this great master (for years I've had the ability to see auras by focusing my attention). I mentioned this to one of my friends, and she replied, "Oh, he pulls his aura in so people can't see it." I was not impressed.

The living conditions there were quite unsanitary. A few years later, on a subsequent trip my friends took, they returned to tell me that the compound was much improved, and the water was drinkable because the teacher was now blessing it at its source. I found out later that the fact was he had installed a water purification system. My husband, David, calls this "magical thinking." My dear friends were blind to any flaws in their guru.

Later it became known that this teacher had some very unholy practices, including being a pedophile! Still people flock to him, being duped. We can so much want a teacher that we ignore or deny the obvious that is glaring at us.

This is what I teach:

1. Do not give your personal power away to any teacher. A true teacher won't want it.
2. Do not check your brain at the door. God gave us the ability to discern and reason. Use it! Trust your inner knowing. Ask yourself, How does this energy feel to me?

You may be asking, How do you find a genuine spiritual teacher? An old adage is, "When the student is ready the teacher appears." And this is true for many on the path. If that does not readily occur for you, join a sangha or a church or a meditation group and see if your teacher is there.

Go on several retreats and see if your teacher is there. Don't cease looking until you find the teacher with whom you fully resonate.

The Fourth Factor is knowing the truth by having our own spiritual experiences. When you reach a clear state of mind in meditation, you know it because you've experienced it. When you see an aura, you've experienced it and you own the experience. When you've practiced generosity and been incredibly blessed as well as blessed others, you know because you've experienced the increased good in your life. You meditate daily and experience greater peace, calm and clarity.

You will know the truth when you experience it for yourself in your own life.

The above is the classic order of the Four Factors. The Dalai Lama has taught that the Four Factors are often reversed for the individual in this manner:

1. We have a genuine spiritual experience. This comes about, as it did for the Buddha sitting under the bodhi tree, from deep inner reflection. We are given a taste of realization. We own it. It is ours.

2. This leads us on our path to develop a conviction to study with authentic teachers, realized beings. For me it has been the Dalai Lama, along with a few others.

3. As we study with an individual, then we are led to seek out great works that will inspire us to go deeper in our studies. As we contemplate these teachings over time, then we are led to just the right books and retreats and courses of study.

4. Our own study and appreciation of the Scriptures themselves develops, and we are drawn to read and study the original material—perhaps even doing some of our own research.

The Buddha said, "Do not believe something to be true because many wise ones say it's true. Do not believe something to be true because I say it's true. Do not believe something to be true because the scriptures say it's true. Believe something to be true because in your heart you know it's true."

In all your spiritual pursuits, learn to listen to your heart and trust your heart, and you will be guided as to what order of the Four Factors is best for you—classic or the reversed.

Don't get selfishly attached to anything,
for trying to hold on to it will bring you pain.

—*THE DHAMMAPADA*

HUNGRY GHOST

THE COSMIC HUMOR is not lost on me as I begin this topic, for I have just begun a several-day fast of warm broth and water. It's too early in the process to actually be hungry, but it is never too early in the process for the monkey mind to begin obsessing over the prospect of possible *future* hunger.

Upon hearing of the concept of Hungry Ghost, I have found the ideas so accurately descriptive and on the mark as to how, in our human mind, we are so similar to a hungry ghost that can never be satisfied.

Consider the image of artist Edvard Munch's *The Scream* with the tiny oval mouth that does not open. The ghostly figure is famished, starving with no means of receiving nourishment, satisfaction or fulfillment of any kind.

As a minister for more than twenty-eight years, I have made many a house call visiting recuperating or ill or elderly congregants. Years ago the awareness came to me that in seeing how one lived—what their homes and cars looked like inside and how they interacted with family—told me volumes that perhaps would not have emerged after years of counseling. I have entered homes, from humble dwellings to mansions, packed with massive amounts of "stuff." I have been invited into rooms that were only narrow pathways in which to traverse the clutter, which included the un-opened boxes of toasters, slow cookers, coffeepots and domed hair dryers and on and on.

On a recent visit to New York City to study with the Dalai Lama, I left RCM Hall late one afternoon. Thousands of attendees poured out onto Sixth Avenue, many attempting to hail taxis. Since it was a bright, warm autumn day, I decided to walk over to Fifth Avenue to try my luck at get-ting a cab there. Well, lo and behold, what was at the corner but Saks Fifth Avenue! Needless to say, I had to go in. I always like to balance my spiri-tual nirvana with a tiny dose of samsara.

I headed directly to the famous new shoe department I had seen on the TV news. It's so large it has its own zip code, if you can only imagine. It was a Saturday mob scene. One would have thought Saks was giving away these shoes, instead of charging prices that ranged from expensive to stratospheric.

I sat on a low bench to take a breather and just observe the frenetic scene when a very young woman approached me. She was tall and stately with beautiful legs that she was attempting to emphasize even more with the elegant stilettos she wore. She asked for my help. Should she buy the plain leather pumps for $400 or the gray snakeskin ones for $875? As gently as possible I—who own many pairs of shoes—explained to her that just minutes before I had been with the Dalai Lama at a lecture and couldn't possibly shift from those teachings and their energy to assist her in choosing between two expensive pairs of shoes. My only advice to this woman of perhaps twenty-two was to ask her to consider how limited would be her opportunities to wear the more expensive of the two pairs of shoes. The black pumps would at least serve her better and longer. She pondered my advice for a moment . . . and then bought the more expen-sive pair! Ah so.

It is perfectly okay to spend our money as we choose. We just need to remember that stuff, no matter how beautiful or expensive, does not make us happy or define who we really are.

A hungry ghost consciousness is one that can never experience any-thing as enough—sweets, acknowledgments, possessions, caring, atten-tion—stuff of any description. Recently I saw an article on a wealthy socialite and her closet, which looked like a fine designer shop. She had 350 coats. Now, even if one lived in northern Norway, what could one possibly do with 350 coats? We all need to learn when enough is enough.

Ponder for a moment the mental clutter that must accumulate over ownership of vast numbers of stuff. How does one remember what one owns? It is mentally draining.

Imelda Marcos and her collection of shoes became legendary. If one has the financial means to own 350 coats, or thousands of pairs of shoes, or numerous house, or airplanes, or are able to do whatever one wants with one's resources, the questions arise: What about their souls? Are their souls satisfied? What are they investing in their souls?

The hungry ghost can never be satisfied but forever attempts satisfac-tion by accumulating, by grasping, by clinging. Other ways the hungry ghost manifests itself is the inability to release and let go. Accumulating or hoarding eventually makes one miserable, causing oneself to suffer rather than offering pleasure. Such activity offers pain.

There are myriad ways the hungry ghost and her phantom character-istics appear. A hungry ghost is:

- The woman at the holiday gift exchange who always chooses the gift she brought out of fear. She believes that if she left her selection to random choice, it would never be as fine as her own purchase.
- The wealthy matron at a luncheon who wins the table arrange-ment, but wants the one at the next table because it looks "fuller."
- The retreatant who, upon receiving blessed beads from the pre-senter of ancient wisdom, goes from retreatant to retreatant ask-ing to switch beads because she sees that theirs would match her dress better.

- The corporate mogul earning millions of dollars a year who attempts to accumulate even more through deception or fraud.
- The alcoholic who no longer even enjoys a drink, figuring that if one beer goes down easily on a summer night, why not twelve or twenty-four?
- The professional athlete who boasts of having sex with more than a thousand women.

The various addictions that entrap people and their lives all have hungry ghost elements to them: the alcoholic, the drug addict, the sexual addict, the food addict, the love addict, the one addicted to being liked. A common denominator in them all is never feeling satisfied, believing that more of the addictive substance is going to provide the magical lift.

Anne, a friend of mine, experienced several years that were most challenging. Her parents, who were in their nineties, became ill simultaneously, as did her husband, much older than she. Her husband was a most successful financier who lived a "John Wayne, I'm in charge, I can do anything, I can make anything happen" sort of life. A second marriage for both, they lived a lavish lifestyle, jetting between their three multimillion-dollar homes.

Anne's husband totally controlled the finances, and that was just fine with her. But toward the end of his life she realized that he had left everything in a trust, with Anne receiving only an annual stipend that was less than what they lived on monthly. She felt that she could return to her previous career as a teacher if he died, even though she had been out of circulation for more than twenty years. She thought she should not say anything, and she did not. When in his last hours her husband questioned the trust he had set up years before, she brushed off his concern and said she would be just fine.

When her husband did pass, his attorneys waited only two weeks to approach her and say she needed to get the primary family home ready to go on the market. This was two weeks after her husband died of a lingering, two-year illness, and eight months after the death of her be-loved mother. Compassion was absent from the communications.

It was shortly after this occurrence that she learned of a highly recom-mended psychic who looked at the photo of a deceased loved one and delivered a message to the living person. Anne brought pictures of both her mother and her husband. Instantly the message came from her mother, "Anne, you have to learn when enough is enough." Anne welled up with tears. These words, this phrase, were the exact words her mother had often spoken to her.

This psychic did not know Anne or her mother. They had never spo-ken before. Anne does not have a hungry ghost personality. She is giving, gracious and generous, definitely not hungry ghost traits. And yet there was a place of fear expanding in her mind. Would she be okay? Would she have enough resources to carry her into the future and beyond? Subtle, hungry ghost thoughts were rising. Fortunately for Anne, she is aware enough not to water those seed thoughts. Yet her mother's message from beyond the grave was, "You have to learn when enough is enough." Anne was quite moved by this message, because it helped her come to the real-ization that she would always have more than enough to meet her every need, as well as delivering to her the most valuable lesson that those who love you will always love you.

Consider where in your life you have perhaps been living like a hungry ghost, never satisfied, always one with an insatiable appetite. Where are the excesses in your life? It may not be accumulating things, but your excesses may be worry, control, power or wanting to be liked or acknowledged.

When visiting congregants in their homes, I have truly seen it all, from simple Zen perfection to unimaginable clutter. Metaphysical teacher and author Terry Cole-Whittaker has a saying that I just love: "Stuff loves people." That always comes to mind when I see a home overflowing with stuff. It really makes no difference if it's expensive, fine stuff or recycled dime store stuff. It is simply too much stuff, too much clutter.

Diane, a friend of mine whom I adore, went through a horrendous divorce where she lost who she thought was her soul mate. She did, however, get to keep all the vast amount of stuff from their 6,000-square-foot home. When she moved into a 2,400-square-foot condominium, all of the accumulated, coordinated, designer-decorated, elegant, expensive stuff came along.

Her new residence looked like a very crowded, high-end furniture store. It was packed to the brim—the walls, the floor, everywhere. There were even sculptures under tables because there was no place else to put them. Diane has always been meticulously neat. Even though her packed house was clean, it was extremely difficult to get from room to room. Nothing could be appreciated because there was so much of everything.

While I was her houseguest for a few days, we talked about what was going on. Diane, a professor, knew this situation was not healthy. But, as she explained, "I'm just not ready to let anything go yet." She added that when she healed from her divorce, she would.

When we saw each other more than a year later at Christmastime, she told me she had taken many items to a designer resale shop and had a sale at her condo. Also, she packed up one-third of what was left and put it in storage for now, and she would have another purging and sale in the spring.

Diane had wrestled long and hard with the dissolution of her marriage and the dismantling of her very comfortable lifestyle represented by her beautiful things, but now she has at long last found the inner beauty of her soul. She has found peace and is so much happier. She is no longer a hungry ghost.

It is apparent that in society today we can all look within and examine just when "enough is enough." To do so brings great release and personal freedom. One can then live without being under the strain of constant accumulation and management. Then you have the chance to clear your mind of all the mental baggage and clutter. To know right now that you are already complete, whole and free is enormously liberating.

Outer clutter in one's life clutters the mind. It is almost impossible to be very effective at mindfulness meditation in the midst of great clutter. Here is a grand technique I heard some folks talking about doing. It sounded great.

First, you need to obtain five or six large, secure boxes with lids. Label each box according to the room you are in. Let's say you are in your bedroom with the appropriately labeled box. In the room you could have:

1. Picture frames and unframed pictures.
2. Mementos.
3. Sweaters.
4. Unworn or seldom-worn jewelry.
5. Clothes that do not fit.
6. Knickknacks and books.

Set aside several hours and systematically go through all the stuff in the bedroom with the intention of de-cluttering. Look at every single item and ask yourself: Is this piece beneficial to me? Do I need it now in my life? If the answer is yes, put it back in its place. If the answer is no, put it in the "bedroom" box and write what the item is on an index card you can keep in an accessible spot. Go through the entire room, remembering the goal is to de-clutter.

When finished you'll have your index card(s) that delineate all the contents. Store the box or boxes, go to the next room and repeat the process until you complete your entire home. After one year, decide if you really want or need what's in those boxes. Keep what you want and sell or give the rest away, circulating your stuff and blessing those who will want it and use it.

I am not suggesting that we divest ourselves of everything we possess externally and internally and go live in a monastery (although at times this idea is tremendously appealing to me, just so long as my husband and our two dogs and one cat can come, too).

I am suggesting that we mentally and soulfully shift from over-consumerism to mindful consumerism, that we realize more is not better, it's just more, that we realize the fulfillment and satisfaction that we desire already exists within our essence, our core. We become full spirits rather than the old, ghoulish hungry ghost.

We then begin to alleviate our suffering through Right View, Right Thought, Right Effort and Right Mindfulness. In studying Buddhism, it has always been important, as in all my spiritual pursuits, to make the connection between the teaching and the practical, day-to-day living of life.

For these extraordinary teachings to have meaning in your life, you must faithfully apply them to your day-by-day, even moment-by-moment, living. Then the shift happens.

The hungry ghost mentality devours its host. The victim of the hungry ghost must find satisfaction, fulfillment and meaning, not in the hoarding and the clutter, but in removing the obscurations that are blocking the awareness of the divine in us—first from the mind and then in the outer environment.

When we have realized our inner Buddha nature and know that part of ourselves, then we can feel safe enough to begin to let go of our stuff. We then gradually learn a valuable lesson: There is always enough!

There is enough of whatever it may be—enough coats (stores in the future will still be selling coats), enough shoes, hair dryers and coffeepots. It can actually be fun to open an unknown holiday package and be surprised.

A recurring theme in Buddhism is that everything one does is for the benefit of other people. Buddhists are the most selfless people I have ever met. They are praying for our happiness right now. They clearly know there is enough for whatever we need without grasping or clinging.

THE ANTIDOTE

The use of Right Mindfulness for freeing oneself from the suffering of the hungry ghost mentality can start with the simple observation of your thoughts and actions. A helpful technique I use is wearing mala beads (the Buddhist prayer beads, 108 in number used to count a chant or mantra or prayer) that are wrapped around my wrist. Many wear them as a necklace. They cause me to pay attention when I reach for something while shopping. Do I really need it? The beads act as my visual reminder not to get sucked into the vortex of "too much."

Continuing with helpful antidotes, we can engage Right View and Right Thought. Here are our deepest perceptions where we can let go and feel safe and cared for and nurtured from within. We find satisfaction in what is. We are at peace. Being at peace allows us to think clearly, free of mental anguish. We no longer think we have to fight and scrape for what is ours. Rather we can let go of the struggle and allow the natural order and goodness of life to embrace us and all others.

We certainly can find benefit in applying any one of the teachings of the Eight-fold Path, but to keep it simple, we will conclude for now with Right Effort. When Right Effort is engaged, you are no longer spinning and grasping, wasting your precious life. Your life energy goes toward what will be truly beneficial to you and others. You are wise enough now to cease looking for happiness and fulfillment where they never can be found.

Using these methods can prove to be very beneficial in freeing your mind from its mental chains, freeing it from the hungry ghost.

The unenlightened mind blames all of its problems
on outer circumstances.

—HIS HOLINESS THE DALAI LAMA

INNER DISARMAMENT

W E ATTEMPT TO CONVINCE ourselves that if he behaved differently, my life would be okay. If this staff, those government officials, that school board, our society were only different, my problems would be gone. Those are thoughts of the unawakened mind. The awakened mind realizes that all external experiences come from one's own mind.

The unenlightened mind is filled with what the Buddhists call "mental afflictions." We might call it dysfunctional patterns or negative thoughts or toxic memories. They are all the same thing, just different languaging. Mental afflictions are states of fear, be it jealousy, rage, revenge, envy, conceit, stress, sorrow, greed, hatred, ignorance, aversion, craving, grasping or attachments. They are all fear-based states.

The source of *all* our problems, according to the Dalai Lama, arises from our mental afflictions. When we are living in the unenlightened mind state—asleep—we think it is all outside of us. We believe we have nothing to do with being the cause of whatever is happening. When we begin to awake, we come to the realization that, without exception, it is all inside of us.

This is also the metaphysical/spiritual view, but applying this teaching 100 percent of the time is extremely difficult and takes years of practice to master. Buddhist teachers often use the term in describing the effort we must exert, as being "strong like a tree." We must be strong like a mighty oak or a California redwood, so when the winds and storms of life come, we (like the tree) remain steady, rooted and certain. We remain steady and certain so that we are never tempted to believe a particularly trying circumstance is the cosmic exception and is outside of us where these great truths do not apply.

There are antidotes to these mental afflictions:

MENTAL AFFLICTION	ANTIDOTE
Fear	Love
Judgment	Compassion
Cravings, Grasping	Gratitude, Giving
Conceit	Humility
Regret	Understanding
Aversion	Acceptance
Attachment	Generosity
Rage	Peace (through meditation)
Revenge	Doing good works

> *If an individual has a calm state of mind, that person's*
> *attitudes and views will be calm and tranquil,*
> *even in the presence of great agitation.*
>
> —HIS HOLINESS THE DALAI LAMA

Here is a technique to release anger. To become calm, meditate on resolving anger by going within to a place of beauty and connect with the earth, beach or forest.

Breathing in, say, *I know anger is here.* (You acknowledge the problem.)

Breathing out, say, *I know the anger is me.*

Breathing in, say, *I know the anger is unpleasant.*

Breathing out, say, *I know this feeling will pass.*

Breathing in, say, *I am calm.*

Breathing out, say, *I am strong enough to take care of this anger. I am steady like a tree.*

Continue breathing and using the above affirmations until you can sense a deep peace. When this has occurred, you know the anger has been dissipated. You may need to do this a number of times, depending on how deeply rooted your anger is.

This exercise offers us a means of truly releasing ourselves from what the Dalai Lama refers to as "our one and true enemy."

We are often tempted to believe our enemy is some person—a relative, a boss, a mother-in-law, the government, the system, an organization, our past, a deceased person from our past. We must be strong in our resolve, like that tree, always to remember that the enemy is not outside us.

All the great teachings are the same. They all teach that it is inside us. When we realize that this is so, then we can do something about the situation. The belief that it is "out there" keeps us forever in the unenlightened mind, planting negative seeds in store consciousness, and stuck in victimhood.

The Dalai Lama made an interestingly humorous point about this: "Even when a person seems particularly difficult for us to deal with, he still has other things in life to do, such as others to annoy. But our inner enemy has nothing else to do but just to nag us constantly. The ego, the inner enemy, has to stay busy." I know such an inner character. Do you?

There are three stages of spiritual practice for overcoming the mental enemy:

1. Refrain from negative action in connection with the mental affliction. Do not allow your ego to take action in an attempt to get even. This takes great mental discipline. Do not focus on it. Do not call and tell friends and relatives how bad it is. Do not gossip about it. Do everything in your power to take your atten-

tion off the problem. You most likely will have to repeat this over and over until you experience a shift.

"Golden Key" the mental affliction. Golden Key is an early metaphysical teaching. What is to be done every time a negative thought arises in relation to this affliction is instantaneously to replace it with a sacred thought. Try using a thought from the Three Jewels. Go back to page 114 and review.

A fearful/negative thought arises. Replace it with a thought of the serenity of the Buddha or Jesus or the Christ within.

A fearful/negative thought arises. Replace it with a thought of prayer or a thought from a sacred text. What I teach people experiencing great hardship is to pick up any spiritual book, open it at random and read for fifteen minutes. Peace will be found in your selection.

A fearful/negative thought arises. Replace it by speaking with your spiritual teacher or a prayer partner. Unity has prayer partners who are available to pray with you twenty-four hours a day. Call Silent Unity at 1-800-NOW-PRAY (1-800-669-7729). This powerful and wondrous prayer line has been operating continuously for almost one hundred years, and it is a perfect connection when you are in need of prayer support.

These are most meaningful and beneficial methods to utilize the power and truth contained within the Three Jewels.

2. Activate the antidotes previously shared and do so mindfully, consciously, practicing again and again and again. Do not grow weary of practicing. Say your current challenge is excessive attachment to your things and money. Practice opening up the purse strings of your life and give generously to organizations and causes you believe in—your sangha, your church, to a

homeless person, to a child selling candy. I always give to the Girl Scouts, but if I am in a sugar-free stage of my life, I tell the little girls to keep the cookies themselves, or give them away, or keep them to sell a second time. Try it. It feels good and comes with no extra sugar guilt. Practice giving generously, and if you are doing so as a spiritual practice, you will soon begin to notice how good it feels and how many unexpected blessings come your way.

3. Practice eliminating all residue energies. Notice them and mentally sweep them away. We do not give attention to these energies so they will not ease their way back into our consciousness and manifest in our lives.

We must have a deep and abiding spiritual practice to be successful in this endeavor. Sometimes the Dalai Lama makes his point humorously. A few years ago while I attended his teaching, he said, "You can't solve your inner problems with a big house, a good car and pretty colors painted on your face! Only through a warm heart and compassion can we solve our inner problems." I enjoy our medium-sized home, my car and having makeup on my face, but none of that could ever define who I am. No lovely stuff can ever define who you are.

When we have these negative mental afflictions, they cause our minds to narrow, our energies to constrict. For example, if a major mental affliction is judgment, and we do not have room in our hearts for people different than we are, then we become very narrow-minded, constantly judging others. We think that for someone to be acceptable, they must be just like us—the same race, same education, same social status, etc. Such attitudes truly cut us off from the richness of a diverse life.

We can now take this teaching to a global level as the Dalai Lama does when he applies it to world peace. "World peace is not going to fall from the sky," he said, "and world peace is not going to rise from the earth. World peace begins with the individual." You are that individual.

When we experience the mental affliction of warring thoughts in our own minds, how can we possibly expect to have peace in our homes, peace in our community, peace in our nation, peace in our world? This is one reason it is so very important to resolve any personal conflicts we may have.

While doing extremely intensive inner soul work with a medical intuitive, my inner ferocious warrior emerged. "He" was quite frightful to my present persona and very different in expression. His modus operandi was to attack, to do battle, most often upon me. It felt like I was being stabbed over and over between the ribs of my back. I suffered from terrible physical afflictions and diseases beginning with the onset of this century. It all stemmed from the force and control "he" once wielded over me. This may seem a bit far out, as it once did to me, but my proof lies in my experiences. After landing in the hospital three times on both sides of the Pacific, after experiencing two hellacious episodes of pleurisy, and after having raging shingles that created a cruel semicircle of painful rash (both outside and in) around my left side, I was willing to take a fresh look at what was going on.

My medical intuitive doctor said it was the residue of a 500- to 600-year-old warrior, a stocky, muscular young man who still lived in me and presented himself in nasty ways, attacking from within and without. The doctor and I did months of work to convince him he had to go.

Where I had once carried warrior energy, it has now been cleansed from me. I no longer need to put on my armor and do battle with the dry cleaner for losing some clothes or with the carpet cleaner for doing a mediocre job. On and on my list could go. In every situation I still communicate what needs to be said and done, not from my warrior, but from a centered, composed part of me. If whatever happens doesn't go as I would like, I now realize it just doesn't matter. I realized I can live a full and happy life without my white cashmere sweater. When I reached that state of mind, the sweater returned!

Living without the warrior is very peaceful. My mind is not crowded with mental afflictions. While vacationing with friends of ours, both longtime warriors, I shared my experience, and they both "got it." John Henry calls us regularly to report on their experiences and to tell us what a difference dropping the warrior is making in their lives.

Many of my generation had to awaken the inner warrior to do what we needed to do in our youth. And in our youth it often served many helpful purposes. The time comes, however, when more skillful means of living our lives emerge. Then the warrior must go.

Those of us in America live in a bountiful land of plenty. When we wage war in our thoughts, how can we expect Iraq to come to a peaceful accord? We expect the Israelis and the Palestinians to stop warring. But have we stopped warring in our thoughts? Have we stopped warring with our families, our colleagues, our friends, with those we dislike, or even with those we say we like or even love?

We have to become mindful of everything we do, because everything we do matters. Our manner of living has an enormous effect on our planet to either continue war or to bring forth peace.

"The concept of war is out of date," said the Dalai Lama, who received an enormous ovation when he made that statement. Earlier he said, "War is organized, legalized violence." Ponder that thought. It is the concept of killing people to bring forth peace that is outdated. We are not living in the dark ages but we so often act as if we were.

Let us remember that the enemy is not "out there." The only true enemy is in us, as our mental afflictions. "We have met the enemy, and he is us," as the cartoon character Pogo stated many years ago. In order to have outer peace, we must have inner peace. When we have inner peace, it leads to peace in our families. When we have inner peace, it moves in our society. When we have inner peace, it moves into our government leaderships. Then we can begin to have global peace. The focus required to bring about such vast transformations is almost indescribable.

Lama Chonam, the young Tibetan monk who so often speaks to my heart, says, "We Americans [he has become a citizen] expect our political leaders to act like they are our spiritual leaders." They are not our spiritual leaders. There may be a spiritual side to some of them, but when they live and act solely from their political natures they often disappoint us. I have expected our political leaders to act as conscious beings, and I used to get quite perturbed when they did not. They do not because they cannot at this point in time. They have not yet discovered who they truly are. May the words of Lama Chonam bring peace to you as they have to me.

At one session I attended, the Dalai Lama asked the twenty thousand people in attendance to join with him in setting a long-term goal. Many of you, along with many in the audience that night, are familiar with setting goals. He asked us to set a long-term goal for demilitarization, for disarmament, for the end of war. If we would join him in setting that goal, then we would end unnecessary suffering, if not in our lifetime, then in the lifetimes of our children or their children.

If we are to have an end to war, be it in ourselves or upon our global stage, we *must* start within our minds and hearts. That is where peace begins. It doesn't fall from the sky, but rather it emanates from within us. This is where we have disarmament. This is where we have peace.

Om, Madna, Padna, Hum

—CLASSICAL MANTRA

THE ETERNAL CONNECTION

THERE IS AN eternal connection between the mantras of the East and the affirmations of the West. Here East meets West.

Mantras are found not solely in Buddhism but in Hinduism and other Eastern religions such as Sufism as well. Mantras are said to be protectors of the mind. Affirmations and their use have become very popular in the West, having grown out of the late nineteenth-century metaphysical movement. An example is, "Every day and in every way I am getting better and better." Over the years that particular affirmation has been altered to say, for example, "healthier and healthier," or "stronger and stronger." Now they are popular in mainstream America as a spiritual tool, as well as a tool to better performance in athletic pursuits and increasing self-esteem, to name two uses.

AFFIRMATIONS—MANTRAS

An affirmation acknowledges the truth in us. Said Charles Fillmore, cofounder of the Unity movement, "When we affirm, it is to hold steadfast in mind or speak aloud a statement of truth." We don't make the statement true by affirming it over and over again. We affirm it over and over again because it is true. The repetition is about steadfastly establishing it in our minds.

The key word here is "steadfast," when life appears to be going to hell in a handbasket. One holds steadfast to the truth of his or her being. This is connecting with the inner essence that is never altered by circumstances. We hold steadfast and do not waver, because when we waver we get wavering results. We remain "strong like a tree."

This establishes in our own consciousness the truth. We do not, cannot, make something true by affirming. But by affirming we are calling forth that within us which is already the truth. Affirmations are the "yes" action of the mind. They lift us out of false thinking into the consciousness of spirituality. In a like manner, a mantra clears the mind of monkey-mind chatter so that the clear mind of truth is available. Deeper knowings and truths then naturally rise into this consciousness.

Science says we can only focus on one thought in any given moment.

As I wrote these words in Hawaii, my husband rushed into the room and said, "Sorry to disturb you, but you must look out the side window." When I looked I saw in all its perfection the full arch of a bright and clear rainbow, all its seven colors delineated. In Hawaii we see many rainbows, and I am so grateful each time that each one holds wonderment and appreciation for me. A rainbow is a visual affirmation of hope of the innate rightness of our world. A bow in the sky is a promise of God's eternal presence.

When we chant a mantra or declare an affirmation, we bring our minds to one-pointedness. One point of focus clears the mind of all the extraneous contaminates. The chatter ceases, and we can pause and exhale and feel peace and calm. I have become quite committed to using mala beads and repeating a mantra the suggested 108 times. One favorite is "Om, Madna, Padna, Hum," which truly clears my mind. If I am feeling troubled or disturbed, I hold the prayer "I seek refuge in the Buddha, dharma and sangha" in my mind. To make it less Buddhist and still engage the same potency, I say, "I seek refuge in the Christ [or God], the spiritual law and my spiritual community." Gandhi's constant mantra for more than forty years was "Rama, Rama, Rama" (God, God, God). These were the final words on his lips as his life force slipped away.

Mantras definitely clear out the mental confusion and return one to one's center. Tibetan monks chant particular mantras, often a sutra, so that their minds do not drop into mental sinking. We in the West affirm, so that our minds do not drop into negative thinking, which is our way of saying mental sinking. This prevents our minds from dropping into the Five Aggregates.

A sutra can be likened to a beautiful prayer that, when chanted over years, can bring enlightenment. When a group of monks chant a beautiful sutra, they really are, we could say, affirming the truth of that sutra in their lives and in the lives of all sentient beings. For this is how they pray, always including all others.

When I feel stressed, a favorite affirmation of mine is, "I abide in the light and joy and peace of God." This is the truth, and when I feel stressed I affirm it often. Let's suppose you are having a really difficult day, one filled with stress and upsets. Instead of declaring "I am stressed" over and over, simply affirm, "I abide in light and joy and peace" over and over. Repeating this will create a shift in consciousness and in your perceptions and experience. Your focus has shifted from the stress to the inner truth of your being, which is light and joy and peace.

We can see the similarities found in the two seemingly different paths. When we look deeply, we can see the common vein of truth running through various spiritual teachings. Of course there are differences in the language and the practice, but the nugget of truth within both is identical.

One of my favorite affirmations that my husband and I have practiced throughout the years is "I love you, God," affirming our love for God, our connection with God. It stills the chatter and reconnects us at any moment we choose to focus on the Divine.

A frequently chanted sutra from the Heart of Wisdom Sutra is:

Form is emptiness.
Emptiness is form.

This sutra is something the Buddhists focus on extensively. I used to not have a clue as to what it meant. Form can be defined as anything in this world of appearance, everything that is impermanent: your clothing, the chair upon which you sit, the table, the floor, the house, the door, etc. The Buddhists tell themselves this and retell it constantly in order to fully come to an understanding that form is empty, empty of any intrinsic meaning. Buddhism suggests you not invest your life or your treasures here, because it is empty.

When an experience feels empty for you, check this out. Have you not attempted to fill it with form, and the whole situation came up lacking? It is empty of inherent meaning. It does not mean anything. On this earth plane we can get so easily confused when we think we are our possessions, our degrees, our lifestyle, our careers, our wealth. The Buddhists keep saying they are all empty. Don't be tricked. *Form is emptiness.* Flip it over and *Emptiness is form.* They are the same.

Anything that does not endure forever is empty. How incredibly freeing this sutra has been for me. It has enabled me to shift my relationship to things. I am not an ascetic in this lifetime, nor have I any desire to be one. I enjoy beauty and creature comforts, but I know from the depths of my being that they do not define me. I have learned in the letting go of my attachments has come the greater and easier flow of blessings and miracles in my life.

Here is a recent example from my life. We had lived in our Ohio residence, a condo on Lake Erie, for fourteen years. My husband, David, said he had a "less than zero desire to move." On the other hand, I had wanted to move and have a home and garden for several years. Then we purchased a second residence in Hawaii. Well, I got my home, even if it was six thousand miles away. I simply let go of the thought of moving. Form is Emptiness. Emptiness is form.

Then three years passed, and on a fluke a realtor from my congregation and I were going to take a look at a nearby home that was on the market. She knew we were not in the market to buy because of David's "less than zero" interest. So we were going to see this house just out of curiosity, and just as we were about to leave, David came home and announced, "Oh, I'll go along. I don't have anything else to do right now."

We arrived at the house for sale, and it was absolutely beautiful, filled with light, with high ceilings, skylights, brightness, openness, airiness, soft colors . . . and David fell for it! He immediately said, "Let's buy it." I was stunned. And to make a not-too-long story shorter, in ten days the deal was closed. We didn't spend six months of our lives looking at possible homes. We did not look at dozens of homes. There was no inner struggle, no angst at leaving our old and lovely condo. There was no attachment, going or arriving.

Our new home is beautiful, inviting, nurturing, serene . . . and it is form. And David and I know it is form. As a metaphysical teacher, I know the principle well. We can have whatever we want. And while having it, we might as well make it pretty and enjoyable. But we don't get attached to it, for therein lies the pitfall.

Jesus said not to lay up your treasures where moths and rust will destroy them. Do not lay up your treasures (those that are truly valuable in your life, in the impermanent, in the illusionary), for they will prove to be empty, and the day will come when we all see the emptiness of form. For some this realization does not come until the moment of death. Often I have witnessed those filled with remorse or still in denial while on their deathbeds. This is truly sad. What were their lives all about? Don't miss your soul's growth in this lifetime by overlooking the truly valuable.

Here is a great shopping exercise. As you are browsing through merchandise, and the thought rises that you have to have some particular thing, just stop yourself and silently affirm, "(Name this thing you want) Form is emptiness. Emptiness is form." Use this mantra to shift your internal perception.

Understanding the union between emptiness and form leads us to an understanding of ultimate truth. This is what it takes to wake up—ultimate truth. Ultimate truth leads to nirvana—a pretty, happy life of love, joy, service, peace, compassion, equanimity, knowing, fulfillment and bliss.

I encourage you to purchase mala beads at a special store that sells holy objects, or go to my church's website, unitygreatercleveland.com. Click on bookstore, and you can order them there. Once you have your own mala beads, which work far better at keeping count than fingers, use them at least once daily. With a short mantra or affirmation, it takes about four minutes for 108 repetitions. These four short minutes to center yourself in the morning can make all the difference in your day and ultimately for the world. Four minutes to center yourself and pray. Aren't you worth four minutes?

As I added these notes to my computer manuscript, I just glanced at the manuscript page number—108—the number of prayer beads on a mala—108—the sacred Buddhist number. I love this kind of cosmic confirmation. May we all get it. May we all be happy.

To me it is much easier to envision a state where there are no
obstacles created by concepts than to see all things as suffering.
I hope scholars and practitioners will begin to accept the
teaching that all things are marked by impermanence,
non-self and nirvana and not make too great
an effort to prove everything is suffering.

—THICH NHAT HANH

THE THREE DHARMA SEALS

ALL TEACHINGS of the Buddha can be brought back to the Three
Dharma Seals at their foundation.

Impermanence is referred to as one of the Three Dharma Seals (core
of the teachings). The other two are non-self and nirvana. All Buddhist
teachings contain these Three Seals. Impermanence is the first Seal, and
for many (including myself) the most difficult. The humanness of us
wants what we enjoy and find pleasurable to go on forever. We even resist
letting go of pleasant dreams.

IMPERMANENCE

I tend to go to sleep early and rise early. One night, after I had gone
to bed early, the telephone rang at 9 P.M. I roused myself into consciousness and answered it. It was my dear younger cousin Grady, who with his
adorable family was vacationing in our ancestral coastal fishing village

where I was staying and writing for the month. We all had had lunch together that day, and we spent the afternoon seeing the sights of this picturesque village. As we said good-bye, we made plans to have dinner the next evening.

As I spoke to Grady, I could hear his wife, Kim, wailing in the background. My heart froze for a moment. Then Grady said they had just received a phone call telling them of Kim's two-year-old nephew's sudden death. He had drowned in the backyard pond. She had just hosted a joint birthday for their son, who turned three, and the two-year-old nephew. Now the unspeakable had happened. I hurriedly dressed and drove over to be with them. We held one another, as raw emotion erupted at Kim's and Grady's loss.

There is nothing quite like the loss of a loved one through death to bring home the truth of impermanence and to shock our minds out of our everyday perception of reality. The death of a tiny child seems so pointless. There is no explanation, and yet if any of this teaching is true, then we must accept the destiny of each soul, no matter how seemingly tragic or untimely.

All phenomena will one day cease to exist. The process of change is a moment-by-moment experience. It is consistently going on. All things have the nature of cessation implanted in them from their inception. This is a very important teaching to ponder. From within the birth is the death.

The infant grows into the toddler, and babyhood is gone. The toddler grows into the kindergartner, and innocence begins to wane. The school child grows into the teenager, and childhood with its wide-eyed wonder is gone. The teen becomes the young adult—now bearing an ever increasing myriad of responsibilities—and the years add up, perhaps the girth expands, hopes bloom and die, and the years roll by until the reflection in the mirror very often becomes startling. Nothing lasts forever: a gorgeous rose, a dream, a controversy, political pundits, feelings, concepts, family structure, the love of your life, children, *you*.

Life is impermanent. The teaching is that if we can deeply understand and accept this and release our attachments to the idea of permanence, we will suffer less (the Second Noble Truth). Nothing in this world will last, including this world. But in this moment we have enough material to work with without worrying about the disappearance of the world at some far-off, distant time.

The lenses of impermanence help us view reality more accurately. I am reminded of the stories of the baby Buddha's (Siddhartha's) early life within the confines of his father Suddhodana's palace walls.

Young Siddhartha only saw flower buds or blossoms, because each night while he slept, his father's servants would pluck any flower that had reached its peak. This way the child would never see a dead flower, or even an old flower or an aging animal or person. His father endeavored to shield Siddhartha from the harshness of this earthly existence. But, alas, this fantasy world could not be maintained forever.

As Suddhodana aged and Siddhartha became a young man, the son set out on a great adventure to see the kingdom beyond the palace walls. On his grand ride he spotted a sick man, then an old man, then a dead man—none of which he had seen before, or had any awareness of their existence and the stages of life. He was puzzled and confused at what he was witnessing. He asked his companion and male servant Govinda what it was that he was seeing. In this way the future enlightened one was introduced to sickness, aging and death. He was introduced to the human condition of suffering and to impermanence.

Thich Nhat Hanh shares some very wise words in *The Heart of the Buddha*: "It is not impermanence that makes us suffer. What makes us suffer is wanting things to be permanent when they are not." Further clarification on this important point comes from Sogyal Rinpoche. I heard him say, "Life is not suffering, rather it is samsara [the endless cycles of birth, life and death within this world] that causes us to suffer."

I invite the reader to explore in her/his own life how the teaching applies. How recently have you suffered as a result of desiring a situation that was changing to remain the same? Releasing our attachments to people, places and things is one of life's more difficult undertakings.

When my mother suffered two debilitating strokes and could no longer navigate the steps of the two-story home my late father had built, we moved her to a condo we owned across the street from where we lived. The task was left to me to go through the home where my father's spirit still filled the rooms and select which items would go to the condo and which would be sold or given away. Waves of sadness rose and swept over me as I looked at and made difficult choices concerning each piece of "stuff" of their lives. *Impermanence.*

Two years later her health deteriorated more to the point where we had to move her out of our condo and into a nursing home. Then we sold the condo, and I had to repeat the process of ridding it of her material possessions. The same sadness recurred, so I sat down and began to consciously breathe deeply, releasing the rising sensation of sorrow. After several minutes the energy was released, and I returned to the task at hand. *Impermanence.*

People ask me how I can deal with impermanence when it rises in my life or the life of a loved one. The best answer I have is to say, "Prayer and meditation." When something overwhelmingly sorrowful occurs in your life, train yourself to immediately turn to prayer. As soon as possible, find a place to go and sit and breathe. Release your sorrow to God, to the Holy Spirit, to Buddha, to your Higher Power along with your feelings, mind chatter and sensations. Do this until you feel the shift. Then remind yourself that what is happening is but a part of the ever-changing flow of life. Train your mind to seek refuge in the Three Jewels: the Buddha, the Dharma and the Sangha.

One of our closest friends was recently and suddenly left by her husband of eight years. I had officiated at their elegant and lavish wedding out of state. They share an intense and demanding professional life, literally traveling the globe to lecture on their specialties. She is world acclaimed, and, although he is well respected, he doesn't receive the accolades she does. I often wondered if there was any hidden professional jealousy. On the morning he awakened her from a deep sleep and handed her a letter saying he was leaving immediately, I wondered again about his real reasons.

She was devastated. This was not a teenage breakup. They are both middle-aged, accomplished intellectuals. This brilliant woman was reduced to an almost mortally wounded ten-year-old. It took her back to when she was ten and her father died, and it brought forth all the pain and loss that caused.

Both of them are dear to my husband and me. They are close friends. When I went to comfort her a few days later, it felt to me like she was grieving over a death. Her pain was so intense she could not function. She canceled all of her many appointments and stayed at home and cried. I felt deeply for her, but I knew there was no way I could take away her pain. When we were together, I suggested she seek refuge in the Three Jewels. She needed refuge. I suggested she choose one and go to it.

We spoke that day on impermanence. She kept saying, "But our marriage was 'till death do us part.'" Of course that isn't always the case. However, such an unskillful departure by her husband seemed like an unexpected death.

She had overcome much loss in her life, and she had to do so again. Although she didn't like the idea at all and wasn't ready to embrace it, I urged her to pray and meditate on impermanence so healing could eventually occur. Such situations cause much suffering and call for the Eightfold Path to be engaged.

Life is not always what we think we ordered or expected to show up. Sometimes the rug is pulled out from under us, and we are lost and baffled. The death of a toddler, a husband walking out, a career collapsing—on and on the beat of impermanence goes.

An associate recently called asking for support with a very perplexing situation in her church. It seems that a congregant who for years had been a trusted ally and a dear friend had without apparent reason or provocation become a completely different person. She was hostile, highly critical, totally nonsupportive, volatile and exhibiting out-and-out aggressiveness. After decades in ministry, my friend and I have learned to see the humor in the most bizarre situations. And, believe me, they do show up. We joked about how unfortunate it was that we did not believe in evil entities (i.e., the devil) taking over a person, because it was such an easy answer to an outrageous situation.

For whatever the woman's reasons at that time, the relationship and her minister changed. What appeared to be a mutually supportive, loving relationship unraveled and was no more. Impermanence at work!

Our executive director's thirty-six-year-old athletic husband became racked with a raging, untreatable cancer. He dwindled to 114 pounds and died, leaving her a widow with three young daughters. Impermanence.

A physician's stable and secure position in the medical community was threatened by several frivolous malpractice lawsuits, all of which were eventually dropped. Even so, his insurance then tripled from its already astronomically high premiums. He had no choice but to sell his share of his twenty-plus-year practice and relocate across the country. Impermanence.

This physician loved his practice, had the respect of his fellow doctors and served his patients conscientiously. He had a network of friends, was active in his community and served actively in his church. In less than a year it came to a halt. It was over. Impermanence.

We don't have to go looking for impermanence. It is waiting to greet us everywhere we turn. I am writing this in a small seaside community where my maternal family comes from and where I lived as a child. All the family that remains here is one first cousin. She is my only living first cousin. When I'm back in my original hometown, occasionally my mind will float back to earlier times, happy times with both my parents and a pair of aunts and several uncles, my maternal grandparents and my cousin Bobby. All that are left are my elderly mother, my two brothers, my cousin Sabrina and Bobby's son Grady.

Impermanence touches every family. Sometimes we may have several years or even a decade or more with no deaths occurring close to us. But no matter how much we pretend in our society that sickness, old age and death can be kept at bay, they cannot. Impermanence shadows each one of us. The teaching is that, if we accept this, we will suffer less when it makes a stop at our door.

We can find the blessing in impermanence if, when we are healthy and strong, we can learn to value our good fortune rather than squander it. Impermanence can cause us to be very appreciative of all of our blessings, be they family, children, church, position, prosperity, good health for ourselves or family or friends, peace, plenty, spiritual connectedness and insight.

Even our deepest and most holy states of being are still impermanent. We can achieve great states of mind and being and live for a while in a state of clear light. But something rattling always occurs. Life makes its outrageous demands on our time and attention, and our elevated state of being collapses into the mundane. Impermanence.

Impermanence and an understanding of it can cause us to value our beloved, our parents, our children, our family and our friends even more. My husband, David, daily engages in the Buddhist practice of meditating on his own death, a practice I have yet to begin. He says that meditating on his impermanence assists him living in and appreciating more fully the present moment.

He finds this meditation to be most beneficial among his spiritual practices. Once several years ago I heard His Holiness the Dalai Lama speak of this practice and his having done it for many years. In his engaging, whimsical way he said, "I have been taught that this will be beneficial at the moment of death, but since at the moment of death I won't be able to tell you if this is so, I'll just have to see!" Then he laughed heartily.

Practicing clinging, grasping and attachment is the antithesis of embracing the Dharma Seal of Impermanence. We cling to what was, and we cause ourselves to suffer. We grasp at what we once had, and we cause ourselves to suffer. We attach ourselves to mistaken concepts and attitudes, to unskilled behaviors, to unconscious people, and we cause ourselves to suffer.

Through these three ego activities we endeavor to keep life like it was. We endeavor to keep the river from flowing, but we cannot stop the flow of life no matter how much we protect or fight our own battle against it. When we awaken to the fact of impermanence, we can then begin to live a more mindful existence, which in turn results in a more loving and joyous life.

A renowned Buddhist teacher, who himself was a teacher of the Dalai Lama and who spent twenty-two years of his life in retreat, said near the close of his life: "When you look deeply, you realize there is nothing that is permanent and constant, nothing, not even the tiniest hair on your body. And this is not a theory but something you can actually come to know and realize and see, even with your very own eyes."

Meditating on impermanence is not something most of us relish doing. We have become very adept at pretending that, if we do not look deeply, we can keep the masquerade going forever, but . . . we cannot. Everything we treasure will one day be visited by the three fellows of sickness, aging, death. This applies to a body as well as to an automobile or your home or the Grand Canyon.

If you have been laying up your treasures in the material world, valuing your "stuff" as though those things have meaning, the day of awakening will come. And if you aren't mindful now and don't endeavor to know a deeper truth, that day can be quite painful.

A dear and beautiful friend of mine, had been, as long as I had known her, Velcroed to her possessions. She believed her "stuff" gave her a sense of self, status and position. Time went by, her accumulations grew, and her husband's accumulations grew. Among her husband's accumulations was a girlfriend living in their second home. My friend was slammed in the face with some very unpleasant facts. Filing for divorce was extremely difficult, for she did love her husband. But she had been in total denial about his extended "business" absences. She did not live in an "equal division" property state and had not been married for twenty years, which would have put her in a better financial position.

To shorten this grim story, she did not fare well in the divorce settlement, in part because she was too traumatized and frightened to stand up to her estranged husband and his powerful attorneys. Her life as she had known it was over. Her husband was gone. Her home had to be sold. Her possessions, besides being divided up, also had to be sold because she was so cash poor. What she had been and what she had possessed was no more.

For the first few months she was inconsolable and considered suicide. Why? Because she had no inner resources. She built her sense of self on outer resources and was quite clueless about any inner world. With the help of family, friends and therapy, she slowly began to crawl out of the black abyss to which she had descended. She did have a good heart, albeit a wounded one. Life forced her to look at her attachments and her clinging and grasping. She was taught a very harsh lesson on impermanence that she is still learning. She thought all her stuff gave her life meaning. Now she is seeking meaning from within through finally finding a spiritual practice, seeking a spiritual community and continuing in therapy.

The teachings on meaninglessness, which I first encountered in *A Course in Miracles*, were a perfect introduction for me to have to grasp impermanence. To learn that nothing has an inherent sense of meaning than to come to understand that with practice it was a tiny leap for my conditioned mind to make into understanding impermanence and emptiness.

The Seed of Impermanence does not mean that we do not treasure life. Rather, a true understanding of impermanence allows us the experience of being truly alive and all that accompanies that feeling. It brings us to a state of mind where we can value every person, each moment, because we know however wonderful, boring or challenging it is, it is fleeting. Don't make the soul mistake of not valuing those you love while they are with you. Love them now. Be kind to them now. Be generous with them now. Treasure them now.

We can learn through pleasure or pain. Unfortunately most of us choose pain. And it was then that through loss, chaos, cheating and deception my friend was forced to learn her lessons. In time it did bring her closer to her core, the love and goodness that was and is in her.

May the profound words of Chagdud Tulku Rinpoche resonate in your heart: "Always recognize the dreamlike qualities of life and reduce attachment and aversion. Practice good heartedness towards all beings. Be loving and compassionate, no matter what others do to you." What they will do will not matter so much when you see it as a dream. The trick is to have positive intention during the dream. This is the essential point. This is true spirituality.

Impermanence Exercise

In meditation do a life review of the 10 Destructive Actions. These ten break down as three physical, four verbal and three mental.

THE THREE PHYSICAL

1. Killing—Most of us are not murderous, so we need to expand and examine how we have harmed others physically. This first point reaches beyond physical combativeness. Have you killed an idea? Another's dream?
2. Stealing—How and in what ways have you ever stolen? Perhaps you have lived out of integrity and have "stolen" the self-esteem of another, or even stolen a colleague's idea.
3. Unwise sexual behavior—Maybe you have been involved in promiscuity, adultery or unkind sexual behavior such as self-gratification with no regard for your partner.

THE FOUR VERBAL

1. Lying—Have you been untruthful in your verbal communications, even just a little? A Hindu teaching is that if one never tells even the tiniest of lies for twelve years, he will achieve enlightenment. How close are you? Why not start today?
2. Creating disharmony—You may have done this through slanderous speech or stirring a pot of discontent that did not need to be stirred.
3. Harsh speech—You do this through the unskilled action of judgmental words by criticizing others, ridiculing others, cursing, swearing, yelling or hurting others' feelings with unkind words.
4. Idle talk—Do you gossip about others, spreading unsubstantiated tales for no reason other than self-aggrandizement? There are spiritual communities that view gossip as one of the most destructive actions of human behavior.

THE THREE MENTAL

1. Coveting—You become the hungry ghost by never being satisfied with what you have, desiring another's good fortune.
2. Malicious or hateful thoughts—We sometimes think in ways that are not only harmful to others, but very deleterious to ourselves.
3. Wrong views—Bigotry and prejudice fall under this category, as you deem people inherently angry, evil, unkind, bad, selfish, etc. (See the chapter on Right View.)

These ten destructive actions lead to great mental confusion and distress. To do this meditative practice properly with adequate focus on each action, you may need to do it in three parts over three days. Practice releasing them until you feel a positive shift in your consciousness and sense your perceptions clearing.

Look at each one of the ten and ask: How has this shown up in my life? How does this apply to me? It may be helpful to have a notepad and jot down whatever arises in your mind.

To deepen this practice you can on another occasion explore how you feel others have directed these ten destructive actions toward you. Practice forgiving yourself and others for whatever arises in order to free yourself from its karmic hold on you.

Repeating this meditation frequently clears out these destructive factors from our minds and the other person's and leads us into having a pure heart. This is particularly beneficial to prepare one to be conscious at the time of death.

NON-SELF

Thich Nhat Hanh beautifully communicates in *The Heart of the Buddha Teachings*: "As long as we see ourselves as the one who loves and the other as the one who is loved, as long as we value ourselves more than others or see ourselves different from others, we do not have true equanimity. We have to put ourselves 'into the other person's skin' and become one with him if we want to understand and truly love him. When that happens there is no 'self' and no 'other.' "

Like certain other Buddhist teachings, non-self is a difficult concept initially for the Western mind to grasp. I generally think of non-self as oneness, although my Buddhist friends tell me it is not exactly the same. It can be more fully explained as emptiness. There is no self that remains the same.

There is no permanent self. We can understand this, because we know every second countless cells are dying and others are replacing them. Thus, we are not *exactly* in the same form from one moment to the next. This is non-self. Nothing is ever separate.

I can understand the concept of separation. Believing we are separate keeps us from knowing the depths of the great spiritual teachings. One can adamantly believe that he is separate from you, from the annoying relatives, from the homeless man on the subway—but the truth is, he is not. This is non-self. Personally I think something has got to be lost in the translation of the word "non-self." Healing the Divide is a Buddhist organization founded by Richard Gere. As the name implies, it is dedicated to assisting us in seeing the oneness of us all.

Those I call annoying are in me. You are in me. I am in you. The homeless man is in me. The radiant child is in me. The flower, the tree, the sky, the ocean is in me. We are all interwoven in the same fabric of life.

Non-self is not a Buddhist philosophy, it is an insight. In our Western thought, when we grasp non-self it is an "aha" moment, a great and profound insight into the fundamental nature of life.

To explain this challenging concept of non-self more fully, I have adapted a teaching of Thich Nhat Hanh in which he explains non-self in a family construct.

Our families are in our consciousness. We carry all the seeds of our particular families in our "store consciousness." We can deny them, attempt to shut them out of our lives, but there they are, lurking in our store consciousness.

I know a number of families in my work and world where an adult son has pulled away and completely rejected his family of origin, usually for no apparent reason. A minor upset or infraction occurs, and "Joey" is gone. It makes no sense whatsoever to everyone in the family. It seems unreasonable. Joey has left no forwarding address. This is not a rare or random occurrence. I know of at least six families where this has occurred. Such family dysfunctions show up everywhere. Oh how we wish it was not so. But it shows us, if we are willing to see, that when we run away we are still carrying our family in us.

Impermanence and non-self can open the doors to reality for us, as we begin to touch all things and all aspects of life deeply. We come to understand that one thing is all things, that one person is all persons.

Many years ago I learned this wonderfully insightful exercise from His Holiness the Dalai Lama, and I have taught it to numerous folks:

"Just Like Me" Exercise
Whenever you cast a judgment upon another person, you train your mind to instantly respond by saying, "Just like me." Examples:
What a cunning person . . . just like me.
What a phony person . . . just like me.
What an egghead . . . just like me.
What a thoughtful person . . . just like me.
What a generous person . . . just like me.
What a terrible driver . . . just like me.
What a self-centered egomaniac . . . just like me.
What a loving person . . . just like me.

A truth I have long endeavored to live and have taught is that it is not possible for us to observe, witness or judge a behavior or trait in another person unless it lives in us. People generally resist this teaching, and some even raise bitter objections. No matter how adamantly they argue, it does not alter "Just like me." If anything, it brings the teaching into greater clarity.

I teach this concept in my first book, *A Course in Love*. There was a woman who was in my congregation years ago who really loathed me (we know she actually loathed herself, even though she focused her venom toward me). For the longest time I could not get a grasp as to why she was in my life. I'd practice forgiving her, blessing her, letting her go, sending her on to meet her good, and she would still be there snarling at me from the front row and taking notes. I later found out the notes were about my wardrobe, not my teachings. She was vitriolic in her hateful words toward me, but she would not evaporate or go away no matter how much I prayed.

Finally I remembered "Just like me." How I was like her was very difficult to fathom initially. So I made a list of her hostile and annoying characteristics, and after each I would say, "Just like me." After a number of repetitions the light began to dawn. She was the outer voice of my inner critic. "Aha, just like me." She would criticize loudly for anyone within earshot to hear, just as I criticized myself at times silently within my own mind.

Through the years I have made enormous strides in that area and have silenced and released the inner judge, resulting in increased freedom and much greater peace and happiness.

"Just like me" is a wonderful and profoundly aware insight to make. We are not separate from our nemesis, no matter how distasteful they are or how much we dislike them.

She was I. I was she.

She finally did go away, but not until my inner work was done and my own inner critic went into retirement.

Years later I was co-officiating with an Orthodox rabbi at the funeral of a member of my congregation who had been raised in Orthodox Judaism. It was very uncomfortable, because several of the family members were literally yelling at one another. At one point, when I was at the podium speaking, the elderly rabbi began raging at me because I was a woman, and no woman had a right to speak at a funeral. The entire situation was ugly and certainly not what the deceased deserved.

Afterward, when the funeral directors and sane family members were apologizing to me profusely, out of my past came this same woman who had been in my congregation. I almost laughed out loud. *Okay, God,* I thought, *is there anything else that could happen today? Bring on the locusts!* Amazingly this formerly angry woman said kind and thoughtful things to me and said not to take on the ragings of the old rabbi. For me that encounter was a miracle.

She is I. I am she.

The raging Orthodox relatives and the rabbi are me, and I am them.

Some races and cultures and religions are completely into separation and the sense of a separate self, never to find any connection with others.

Other races and cultures and religions look for the similarities and seek to recognize the inter-being, the non-self.

"Just like me." What we perceive, we are.

What I saw in the rabbi was fear, fear that his tightly controlled world was coming unraveled by my presence as the leader at that time. I knew the deceased well. The rabbi had never even met him. The rabbi is an Orthodox Jew. He saw me as a Christian (not how I define myself) and female. From his viewpoint it was absolutely blasphemous that I would be present, let alone leading the service. It was inconceivable to him that the deceased, one of my favorite congregants, a precious elderly man, would be attending Unity with his son. So he was in fear. "Just like me." When in fear, attack is a common response. My presence became like a lightning rod. By my very presence I was saying, *We are one.*

With non-self we are all waves in the great ocean of life. Non-self helps us begin to see all as our brothers and sisters—from the Dalai Lama to Uncle Ed, to your mother-in-law to the grocery store clerk—as one. This in turn gives us not only great insight but also great compassion for others.

When we have developed the ability to look deeply, we can begin to see that there is no separate, independent self. We see how we are interconnected with all beings. Many people live just to satisfy themselves, not realizing that in living to bring happiness and joy to others, they will attain happiness and joy themselves.

I visited my mother's cousin Margie, who lives about twenty miles from where I was writing and whom I had not seen for a number of years. She is a tiny, sweet, dear woman, now a widow living alone and in the early stages of Alzheimer's disease. When she first saw me, she thought I was my mother. Throughout our visit at various times she thought I was all of the women in my mother's family, including my grandmother, who left this life forty years ago.

She was very chatty remembering with joy all kinds of tales from the past, saying, "You remember Theresa. We all went to school together." Gently I'd remind her, "No, that was my mother." Then we decided to call my mother, who she soon thought was my mother's mother.

As we continued to visit, I began to see the energy of non-self dancing about the room and within our conversation. Cousin Margie's brain had the female lineage of her family intact, but the individuality was no longer discernible to her. She didn't introduce females from the old neighborhood or relatives from her father's or husband's side. There was simply a fading and a blending, and in her mind my grandmother, aunt, mother, her sister and I became one person.

If we all could see life that way and then multiply it by a billion, then we would be getting close to non-self, oneness, emptiness.

His Holiness the Dalai Lama speaks of our "grasping at self existence," that this is "an erroneous belief that keeps us imprisoned in the cycle of existence," which is to say, samsara—birth, life, death, rebirth, again and again. All of life is impermanent and without self. We can eventually develop profound insight to deeply touch all of life without self and become free from birth and death. We can become free from impermanence and permanence, as well as free from non-self and self. Only then do we arrive at the Third Dharma Seal, Nirvana.

NIRVANA

A wanderer spoke to the venerable Sariputta: "Reverend Sariputta, it is said, 'Nirvana, Nirvana.' Now what, your reverence, is Nirvana?"

Reverend Sariputta replied, "Nirvana, it is said, is formless. It has always been. It was not created in man. It cannot die. The way to Nirvana can be pointed out, but it would be impossible to show a cause for the production of Nirvana."

Nirvana is our true, ultimate expression of being. I heard Thich Nhat Hanh teach that Nirvana means "extinction." Now this is where the Eastern mind and that way of teaching is very different from the Western mind.

How can it be defined as "extinction"? All normal beliefs, concepts, ideas, perceptions become extinct with Nirvana. Our perceptions fill our minds and keep us in ignorance. On our way to awakening, we have to rise above our notions, concepts and perceptions.

In Nirvana we touch our real self, our non-self, our profoundly spiritual nature. This true self is what we can learn to touch—the ultimate nature of reality. Nirvana is the ground of being of all that is. In metaphysics this profound state of being is called Christ consciousness, illumined consciousness, when we are truly at our essence. We are in our Buddhahood.

Nirvana is the extinction of suffering. It is our notions, concepts, attachments and perceptions that cause us to suffer. When we give these up and silence our monkey mind, our suffering begins to diminish, our joy increases, our state of awareness is clearing, and we are waking up and reaching Nirvana.

In Nirvana we know we have already had all along what we were searching for. We are what we have always been. We touch our true nature.

The greater truth is that we need do nothing. What in the world can that mean? It is absolutely a Buddhist principle. We do not need to run here to there, rushing about in our quest for enlightenment. We do not need to search anywhere. All we need "do" is turn within. Here lies the vast reservoir of our true self. Just being our authentic self is enough. And yet there are many paths and methods and schools and practices to get us in touch with our authentic selves.

I perceive all of the above as a means of discarding our unknowing to reach our knowing. We can carry around a shipload of unknowing, false knowings, mistaken concepts, beliefs and perceptions.

A Buddhist term that is used here is "aimlessness," again difficult for the Western, educated mind to understand. Often the meaning is lost in translation and convoluted in its character.

From the *Dhammapada*: "There is no fire like lust, no sickness like hatred, no sorrow like separateness, no joy like peace. No disease is worse than greed, no suffering worse than selfish passion. Know this and seek Nirvana as the highest joy."

Says American Buddhist scholar Robert Thurman, ". . . realization of Nirvana transforms the ordinary, relative world into an extraordinary, perfect environment or 'Buddhaverse'" (Thurman's term for what is generally called Buddha-land). Imagine living in a Buddhaverse. How would life be different for you? For all of us?

In Nirvana we are free from all concepts and notions. In Nirvana we have had and continue to have our own direct experiences of blissful reality. Theory does not result in Nirvana. Actual experience and deep practice is what can bring one to this remarkable state of being. No one person or teaching can take your experience from you. It is now your very own. You own it.

We know what we know, and we do not know what we do not know. An example I often use to illustrate not knowing what I do not know is that I've never had a baby. I have not given birth. It does not matter how many times I have seen actual births on video or in person. I DO NOT KNOW what giving birth is like psychologically, physically or spiritually. There is not a man on the planet, including all male ob-gyns, who knows what giving birth is really like. One has to have the experience to know. So therefore we can only truly know what we have experienced and do not know what we have not experienced.

Entering the Threshold of Nirvana

Nirvana is the state of awareness of all that is. One of my remarkable, blissful experiences came in the mid-1990s while studying with His Holiness the Dalai Lama in Los Angeles. It was several days into the teaching when my dear friend Linda and I arrived at the UCLA auditorium early in the morning to be present when His Holiness would be doing his morning chanting aloud.

She and I stood in place for twenty or more minutes, drinking in this remarkable energy. After the chanting, the morning session was to begin and we returned to our seats next to my husband, David, and our friend Roger. As the session began, something very out of the ordinary began to occur in my mind and body. Every cell and atom began to vibrate with light, and I began spontaneously to go into a profoundly altered state. With each passing moment the experience accelerated.

Linda was acutely aware something was going on within me and asked if I needed to go to a quiet place. We left and returned to the hotel. In my room she proceeded to work with the burning energy that was radiating from my entire body, concentrated between the second and fifth chakras as a great turning wheel spiraling out from me and emanating from above me.

I was not afraid. I had had some experience with what can happen in extremely deep and profound meditations, but the earlier experiences paled in comparison to what was then occurring. It felt as if my entire electromagnetic field was undergoing a cosmic tune-up. It was like I was moving out of a human experience into something other, something beyond.

Thank God, I have a husband and friends who have seen beyond the veil and could hold the space, so to speak, for this transformation to run its course. I stayed in this state for approximately twenty-two hours. It slowly began to subside after dawn on the second day. I told our Tibetan friend Lama Chonam and American Tibetan Buddhist translator Sangye Khandro what I had experienced. Lama Chonam responded that he had heard about such occurrences but had no direct knowledge of them. I now do. I experienced it.

For me that experience of opening and awakening so distinctly to bliss for almost a full day was, I dare say, entering the threshold of Nirvana.

At a later teaching of the Dalai Lama, he stated, "Nirvana comes after mind has been thoroughly cleansed of all mental pollutants. The mind is then totally free. This is true Nirvana."

THE THREE DHARMA SEALS, the teachings of impermanence, non-self and Nirvana have been likened to a raft to travel upon to get to the other shore.

|

What you give is what you receive more quickly
than the signal sent by a satellite.

—THICH NHAT HANH

THE SIX PERFECTIONS

THE CHINESE CHARACTER for perfection translates as "crossing over to the other shore." This shore is the shore of liberation, freedom and peace.

Visualize how it is now that we spend so much of our lives on the shore of separation, obfuscation, stress, disease. We all spend time there. Here is a formula that affords us the opportunity to cross over from the shore of separation to the shore of liberation. When we are focused and committed, we can actually do this with amazing ease.

This technique is a daily, moment-by-moment practice. For all Six Perfections we begin by centering ourselves through our breath. Stop and take three deep breaths, slowly, in and out. By doing so we become centered and begin to cross over. Said the Buddha, "Just don't hope that the other shore will come to you if you want to cross over to the other shore—the shore of safety, well-being, freedom from fear and anger. You have to swim or row across. You have to make an effort." This is the Buddha's way of saying you have to do it for yourself.

Here is a formula using the Six Perfections to get to the other shore. The six are interdependent.

GENEROSITY, THE FIRST PERFECTION

If one is tight and stingy in one's thoughts, money, time, attitudes, possessions, this First Perfection is telling you that you are not ready.

A most important step is to convey generosity of spirit, so that we become generous with supportive, kind, loving words. We are generous with our attitudes, being slow to judge or criticize. We become individuals who are quick to have compassion, to be kind, to express loyalty, to give of our time, talent and treasures when the offering baskets of life are passed. We are generous with our willingness to celebrate another's good. We are genuinely delighted at another's good fortune.

As we develop this First Perfection, what has to occur is that great good must flow into our lives. As stated in *A Course in Miracles*, "Into the hand that gives, the gift is given."

A little boy of a very wealthy father was asked by the dad, "Honey, what do you want for your birthday?" The little fellow thought for a moment, then told his father, "Daddy, I want you."

Giving is a vital part of Buddhist practice, as it is taught in Judeo-Christian spirituality, but not so often practiced. It still baffles me how resistant Westerners can be to the spiritual practice of tithing (giving back 10 percent of your income to your spiritual home or sangha). The successful and happy people I know live this principle. Those who struggle do not, yet they are fearful and resistant to personally engage in a practice that has worked and continues to work for so many through the ages.

A most prosperous and extremely generous friend of mine, Alice, always has sincere people coming up to her, wanting to meet with her and ask a question—always the same question. "What is your secret? What is the one thing you do that you can attribute your success to?"

Alice always responds, "Giving. It is and has always been through my giving that I have prospered." She humorously relates that the folks who ask the question almost never accept her answer. They will summarily brush it aside and say, "Well, yes, but what else?" For Alice there is no other answer. She sums it up by saying, "People want another answer!" They want to get where Alice is, but they don't want to give. Until they hear her message, they will never come close to where she is.

We give so that others may experience happiness. When others are mean, selfish or unkind, being generous with our love is an important antidote. When another's behavior is unkind or harsh toward us, it is because that person is suffering. If we are very awake and aware, we quickly realize this individual is calling for our compassion, not our rejection. We offer compassion because we know he must be suffering deeply to behave so poorly. His suffering is spilling over. And when we are within his sphere, it spills over upon us.

When we are truly engaged with this First Perfection, then our spirit is generous with a person—generous with loving-kindness, with compassion, with tenderness, with kind words. We are generous instead of throwing him out of our hearts. He does not need punishment, he needs help and is asking for our love.

Thich Nhat Hanh gives this amazing suggestion: go shopping for that person, not as a manipulative move but rather as a magnanimous gesture. Purchase something that person would absolutely love, a kind response to their call for help. Now that is a generous act from a generous spirit.

Last Christmas I took this teaching to heart and purchased a beautiful scarlet cashmere sweater for a relative whom I love dearly, but who was suffering greatly. He had walked away from his family and friends with much anger and rage, leaving those in his wake very upset and confused as to what had happened.

I prayed and prayed with no outer reconciliation. With the holidays approaching, I then read Thich Nhat Hanh's above message, purchased the sweater and sent a card that expressed my love along with a written invitation to Christmas dinner. We even set a place for him, thinking surely he'll return for Christmas (how could he miss Christmas?), a holiday he has always loved.

to do. Pray? Yes. Have compassion? Yes. But what about witnessing a child being abused? The next day I spoke with several professionals—a child advocacy attorney, a police officer and a social worker. They all gave the same advice. Do not approach the person, but immediately call for help. From that day to this, I carry the Child Protective Services telephone number in my wallet. Now I know what to do. You can do the same thing and get the number for the appropriate agency in your area.

- Deep listening and loving speech. While training for the ministry, we were taught how to listen on two levels: (a) what was being said; (b) what was not being said—the message beneath the words. When we listen deeply, we learn much about another person. It takes much practice, but we all can learn to "hear" the unspoken words behind the spoken ones and "hear" the truth of a given situation.
- Mindful consumption. Use what you use. Use what you need, but don't abuse the generosity of the Universe. In other words, be mindful about everything you consume, from natural resources—water, gas, electricity, etc.—to paper and plastic bags. Begin to have less waste in your household.

INCLUSIVENESS, THE THIRD PERFECTION

In order to practice inclusiveness we must have a huge heart. Your heart is large enough to draw that person and his energy into your heart—receiving, embracing and transforming.

The way the Buddha illustrated this teaching was to imagine we have a heart as big as the ocean. And into that vastness all can enter. If we take a small handful of salt and put it in a bowl of water, the water would not be drinkable. But if we put the same amount of salt into a crystal clear river, the water still remains drinkable. If some salt from a troubled person comes in, it will have no effect because we are as that clear river, or as big as the ocean.

One has to be most generous of spirit to practice inclusiveness.

ENTHUSIASM, THE FOURTH PERFECTION

We must put joyous effort into our spiritual practice. We don't grow weary even when we don't see the desired results. We continue to practice enthusiastically. We plant seeds of joy and happiness in our soul's store-house, and they gather there and are stored for future use. We continue to always water these seeds. This requires the power of spiritual strength to not grow weary—to faint not. I always keep on keeping on. It is a stellar spiritual quality for all of us.

In this store consciousness there are many seeds, seeds of agitation, seeds of negativity. On the other side are seeds of love, compassion, goodness, generosity. We all have both kinds of seeds within us from our past actions and past lives, but it is absolutely up to us what kind of seeds we are going to water. We always have a choice as to what seeds we water. Thich Nhat Hanh says that if we have people in our lives who just love to water those negative seeds—and we all do—they water those seeds of negativity even when we attempt not to let them affect us. He asks that we say to such an individual, "Dearest one, please refrain from watering those seeds." Can you imagine saying that to another? You may choose to do so silently.

Then we water and nurture the wholesome seeds. We use our power of prayer and affirmation to release the negativity and water the positive. Then we cross over to "the other shore" of peace, happiness and liberation.

MEDITATION, THE FIFTH PERFECTION

This Perfection is a two-step process. First we stop the monkey mind within us by deep, slow breathing and centering ourselves. Second, we look deeply within our own mind and into the nature of things. We eventually do everything in our lives mindfully as a result of regular meditation. There are two types of meditative practices. One is learning to become still and centering the mind. The other is the conception process of reasoning. (See chapters on Right Mindfulness and Right Concentration.)

WISDOM, THE SIXTH PERFECTION

Our insight and understanding carries us to the other shore. We look deeply and we have an insight. "This is it! This is what I've been doing, this is what I have not been doing, that keeps me on one shore or carries me to the other." Wisdom can be equated with Right View from the Eight-fold Path.

Buddha taught that the ground of being of all waves, be they tiny or enormous, is the ocean. We, too, have a ground of being that can be called our divine nature. In the West we call it "God," or "Christhood." In the East it is called "Buddhahood" or "Nirvana." This is our true nature, the ground of our being. We don't have to go somewhere to find it. We don't get it someday if we become very, very holy. It is there. It has always been there, and it will forever be there as the ground of your being in the ocean of divinity.

Remember that these precepts work together. They are interdependent. They move us from a state of separation to a state of liberation. They move us to wholeness, freedom and holiness.

At a Rigpa retreat I attended with Sogyal Rinpoche, he taught something I have found to be very helpful, since it fits so perfectly with this sixth Perfection. It is to keep what this master teacher calls an "Insight Journal." You maintain a special little journal that you always have handy.

And when you have a flash of insight, an "aha" moment, you immediately record it in your journal. I faithfully do this, and it is an enormous help in always coming up with fresh Sunday lesson ideas. The Insight Journal is something I truly appreciate.

We all have flashes of pure knowing, but we so often and so quickly forget them. Having an Insight Journal must have been an insight of Sogyal Rinpoche that has now benefited so many people. If you keep one, it will greatly benefit you and help carry you to the "other shore."

In the limitless sea of samsara, in the midst of change, there is an island, a farther shore, a realm of being utterly beyond the transient world in which we live: Nirvana.

—THE BUDDHA

THE OTHER SHORE

EKNATH EASWARAN writes that the Buddha became "a kind of cosmic ferryman." He is represented as always calling: "Koi paraga?" (Anyone for the other shore?) So how do we, as women and men of the twenty-first century, get to the other shore? And, exactly what is "the other shore"?

One could say that it is arriving, not at a physical place, but rather at a mental place that is free of suffering, attachments and fears of any form. On "the other shore" we live in our Buddha mind. We experience literal liberation. We are awake to our Buddhahood, our Christhood. We know what it is like to live on the gross, common shore, and we have done lifetimes of spiritual work and practice. We now desire to cross over into living a more awake, godly, aware life, free of the traps and pitfalls of mundane existence.

Perhaps we have glanced at the other beings who seem to be more peaceful, more tuned into the flow of life, more luminous. And we, too, desire more than anything else what they are demonstrating. It means leaving the familiar shore of suffering and drama behind, leaving behind all that's familiar. Few are willing to do that.

There is a quite revealing opening line in *A Course in Miracles* that has brought such insight and clarity to my mind. It is: "All are called, but few answer." Consider that for a moment. "All are called" rather than the old thought and belief, "Few are called." You have been called to the other shore. "Koi paraga?" Are you willing to answer the call, to do what is necessary to make this life-altering and life-affirming journey?

Many deny the call, reject the call, ignore the call. All the while the call continues. The image comes to mind of a phone ringing endlessly in the background while the meaningless business of life takes precedence. Then one gets farther and farther removed from the ringing, lost in samsara, the suffering of the world, living the painful life of separation, rather than rising up into the wholeness that is being offered, rising into one's holiness and getting on the ferry for the other shore.

My mother is now elderly and has suffered greatly from the loss of her husband, my father, and the two strokes she has experienced. Her pain is compounded by some deep family difficulties. In earlier, stronger times she was a demanding, commanding force to be reckoned with. She was forever the lioness with her three cubs. When I was in Unity ministerial training in Lee's Summit, Missouri, we would talk on the phone at least twice a week. I will forever remember one conversation, perhaps the only conversation I can recall from so long ago.

It was a most intense and stressful time for me during my first year of studies. All that had previously been held dear by me was unraveling. I was living in the questions of what is real and what is illusion. I was exploring the validity of my previously held beliefs. And I wasn't sure I had a grasp on either. In the midst of this mental whirlwind my mother called. She could tell by the tone of my voice that something was not right.

"What's wrong?" she asked.

"Oh . . . nothing that I could actually describe to you, Mom," I replied weakly.

Concern rose in her voice. "What do you mean you can't describe it to me? What's happening?"

"Mom," I stammered. I tried to calm myself. "It is just so bizarre. It's frightening and confusing. It's just bizarre! It's surreal!"

"Joan," she replied firmly, "I do not like the words you are using." Then with sincere concern she asked, "Are they brainwashing you?"

I paused for several long moments before I answered. "Yes, that's it. They are brainwashing me—not in the World War Two or Vietnam tiger cage sense—but it is brainwashing nevertheless." The realization had struck me that every single thought, belief, idea, perception, concept rising out of me was being scrutinized . . . by me. As each one arose, I would be forced to ask: Is it factual? Is it helpful? Is it meaningful? Is it valuable? Is it beneficial? Is it true? If the answer was "no" to any of the questions, I was encouraged to let them go. So, yes, I was being brainwashed, but in a most spiritually sound manner. The experience was like my gray matter daily being removed from my skull and purified by crystal clear water, washing away all my false concepts, cherished beliefs and erroneous notions.

So, yes, Mom. I was being brainwashed in order to discover that there was another shore, then later, after many years of a devoted and intensive spiritual practice, to be able to catch that mystical ferry to the other shore.

Asked what he taught, the Buddha responded, "What do I teach? Whatever is fascinating to discuss, divides people against each other, but has no bearing on putting an end to sorrow. What do I teach? Only what is necessary to take you to the other shore." Oh my God, I love that!

What is life like on the other shore? The seemingly evasive answer is that one has to experience it oneself to know. And that is true. But generally it is leaving separation behind to experience oneness with all. It is releasing in harmony to know peace. It is knowing serenity, contentment, caring and generosity. It is the wonder of having exactly what you need when you need it without struggle. It is giving up effort and instead allowing the Universe to support you. It is what Jesus taught about living in the Kingdom of Heaven. The Kingdom of Heaven can be likened to the Other Shore. It *is* the Other Shore.

Few believe this is possible, few answer the call, but to those few who do the hitherto unimaginable becomes real. How? By living each aspect as taught in the Eight-fold Path. By practicing compassion, generosity, loving kindness. By substituting yourself for others. By faithful daily spiritual practices. By cleansing the scales from your eyes and seeing the beauty that surrounds you. By opening yourself to boundless happiness. It also means giving up the drama and struggle and removing yourself from unhealthy and unwholesome situations and people. Ultimately it means to conquer the whole field of mind to become a Buddha or Christ.

From the *Dhammapada*: "Keeping company with the immature is like going on a long journey with an enemy. Therefore, live among the wise, who are understanding, patient, responsible and noble. Keep their company like the men moving among the stars."

The wise live on the other shore. The foolish ones are unaware of the possibility of more. It is true that those living on the original shore can be very annoying in their endeavors to keep the seeker from catching that ferry, as they continue to pretend the illusion is real. The one who catches the ferry is a threat to the ones who would rather stay in their misery. Says Robert Thurman, "Western society is intolerant of people being happy." You know the old cliché "Misery loves company." The miserable ones do not want you to leave them and cross to the other shore.

Someone else's opinion or belief is never a reason to stay on the original shore. In fact, there is *no* reason to stay. You must answer *your* call, do *your* work, catch *your* ferry, and live in the possibility of boundless happiness on the other shore to become a Buddha. Choose your Buddha nature over what the throngs are doing and how they are living. Always choose Buddhahood.

Time and space will continue to exist, but the enlightened being knows it's not real to him, although it is still real to other people.

Take all this material and spiritual information, digest it, make it your own. Allow it through practice to become your living truth, your soul's knowing, so that you may know that the great and vast truths of Buddhism are as important and relevant today as when the Buddha walked the earth. May we all know that the lotus of eternal truth still is rising out of the mind stuck in the mud of the world of samsara. See in your mind's eye the lotus rising through the illusion. And the lotus still blooms.

May you be filled with loving kindness.
May you be well.
May you be peaceful and at ease.
May you be happy.
And may you cross to the Other Shore.

Glossary of Terms

Affirmation: A short, positive prayer statement declaring as already accomplished a desired good.

Ascetics: The early companions of the historical Buddha who believed an austere life would lead to enlightenment.

Asleep: The mental state of most people while living in samsara.

Bardo: The state we enter immediately upon death. It is an in-between state, where Buddhists believe most remain for forty-nine days.

Beginner's Mind: Young practitioner uncluttered with many concepts.

Bodhichitta: The energy of compassion, grace, love and goodness combined. The supreme medicine.

Brahma: God of the faith practiced by people at the time of the Buddha.

Buddha: The first enlightened being who reached the pinnacle of perfection and evolution. The term generally refers to the historical Buddha of 2,600 years ago.

Chakras: One of seven primary energy centers found in the body, running from the root to the crown of the head.

Clear Light: A term translated from the Sanskrit that means the subtlest light that illumines one's reality or the entire universe. It is different from the light of celestial bodies. It is transparent rather than bright.

Consciousness: The sum total of all thoughts, feelings and emotions.

A Course in Miracles: A twentieth-century spiritual text offering a systematic method for awakening.

Dakinis: Holy, enlightened women of the celestial realms. They move about in the space of absolute reality.

Darshan: A group sitting in meditation.

Deer Park Sermon: Location of the historical Buddha's first teaching in which he taught the Four Noble Truths.

Dhammapada: A sacred collection of the sayings and teachings of the historical Buddha.

Dharma: The entire body of Buddhist teachings. The reality of truth.

Diamond Sutra: The earliest teaching on how to respect all forms of life. The Diamond Sutra reminds us of the great teaching: "Where there is perception, there is deception."

Eight-fold Path: The fullness of the Four Noble Truths. A formula for spiritual awakening. All eight are equally important.

Eknath Eswaran: A gifted teacher of mysticism who came to the United States in 1959 as a Fulbright scholar. All of his writings are highly recommended.

Enlightenment: An instantaneous experience of total awakening from the world of samsara. Sleeping levels of consciousness enter full awakening upon reaching enlightenment.

The Five Aggregates: Containing everything found in nature, in the world at large, and inside and outside of us, the Five Aggregates are form, feelings, perceptions, mental formations and consciousness.

The Four Factors: The very nature of an enlightened person. They constitute a general spiritual practice. See The Four Immeasurables.

The Four Immeasurables: So called because the vastness of their splendor cannot be measured, they are love, compassion, joy, equanimity. Also called The Four Factors.

The Four Noble Truths: The first teaching of Buddha, which set the wheel of dharma in motion. See page 12.

The Golden Key: A creative thought offered by Emmet Fox in which one thinks about God rather than one's own problems.

Happiness: What all sentient beings desire.

Heart Sutra: The teaching of absolute truth in which there is no birth and no death. It is not in contradiction to earlier relative truths. It simply comes from a deeper level of understanding. The Heart Sutra is exquisitely chanted by a sangha of Tibetan Buddhist monks and nuns.

Hungry Ghost: An inhabitant of the so-called hell realms. One who can never be satisfied.

Illusion: The which appears real, but in actuality does not have any enduring reality.

Impermanence: The Buddhist view that nothing in this world is permanent.

Karma: The eternal cyclical law of life. Similar to but not the same as cause and effect.

Lama: A highly trained spiritual teacher.

Mantra: A sound or chant used to save the mind from distractions. Mantra literally means "saving the mind."

Medicine Buddha: The manifestation of the healing energy of all enlightened beings. It can also be called "Spiritual Medicine."

Meditation: Various methods to still the mind and ultimately reach one-pointed awareness.

Metaphysics: A deeper view of all of life that embraces more than just the physical.

Middle Way: A middle or balanced approach to life taught by the Buddha. Not too rigid, not too slack. Sometimes called "Middle Path."

Nirvana: The permanent rising out of all lower states of consciousness or samsara. To dwell constantly in this elevated mind, one's nature is merged into Buddha nature.

Noble Being: One who cares and values others as much as oneself.

Non-Self: The Second Dharma Seal, a challenging concept for the Western mind. It is not quite "oneness." It is not a philosophy, it is an insight.

Om, Madna, Padna, Hum: The most popular mantra (or prayer) that erases and purifies negative emotions and suffering.

Perception: What we individually perceive as the truth, which may not be. Our perceptions may be true or false, and often lead to deception.

Ram Dass: A noted spiritual teacher who, as a young Harvard professor, traveled to India, found his guru and transformed his life. In the ensuing decades he has assisted millions through his clear, direct teachings. His book *Be Here Now* is a spiritual classic.

Refuge: A place of solace for spirit, soul and body. Refuge can be found in the Three Jewels.

Right Action: Having every action be in accord with inner essence. Conscious action.

Right Concentration: Cultivating a mind that is single-pointed.

Right Effort: Using your energy in only life-affirming ways.

Right Livelihood: Having one's career in alignment with spiritual essence.

Right Mindfulness: Living in an awake, aware, conscious state.

Right Speech: Speaking only words that are true, beneficial and in accord with inner essence.

Right Thought: Recognizing and experiencing our true thoughts. Thinking in alignment with the greatest truths.

Right Vew: Perceiving all of life clearing and as it truly is. Looking deeply.

Rinpoche: A highly educated lama who has passed many tests after years of study. The designation can be likened to that of Ph.D.

Samsara: The myriad complexities of life with all of life's lures and illusions. The endless cycle of birth, life and death and being stuck in that cycle.

Sangha: A community of spiritually minded people, often ordained clery, that studies and practices the Dharma.

Seeds: Thoughts held in the mind.

Shantideva: The eighth-century Buddhist master of compassion. His prayer:

> *For as long as space exists*
> *And sentient beings endure,*
> *May I too remain,*
> *To dispel the misery of the world.*

His classic, *A Guide to the Bodhisattva Way,* has instructed for 1,300 years.

The Six Perfections: Six goals, ranging from generosity to wisdom, that enable one to cross over to the other shore of liberation, freedom and peace.

Store Consciousness: The information that fills the subconscious mind.

Sutras: Ancient sacred verses, which are most often chanted.

Tara: Several incarnations of the divine feminine found in Buddhism. The name "Tara" means "she who liberates." One of myriad awakened beings who love and care for others.

Thich Nhat Hanh: A Zen Buddhist monk from Vietnam who now resides in the Dordogne region of France. He is regarded as a profound and perceptive teacher of Buddhism, and is the author of more than forty books.

The Three Dharma Seals: Impermanence, nonself, and nirvana. These three need to be present in any teaching in order for it to be considered true. Understanding that impermanence and nonself, teachings on time and space, lead to nirvana, liberation.

Three Filters of Consciousness: Emptiness, signlessness, aimlessness. They liberate us from fear, confusion, and sadness. Also called "Three Doors of Liberation."

The Three Jewels: Buddha, dharma and sangha. Here we take refuge. These three are a fundamental practice of Buddhism.

Tonglin: Tibetan for giving and receiving. An eleventh-century meditation practice.

Truth: That which never changes, which is eternally the highest spiritual teaching.

Tulku: A child emanation that is pure and noble; recognized by adult lamas as being the return of a previous enlightened one.

Wheel of Dharma: A teaching by the Buddha in the Deer Park Sermon, setting the wheel in motion.

About the Author

Best-selling author Joan Gattuso brings deep, personal insight to all her writing. Her in-depth studies with His Holiness the Dalai Lama have given her the necessary background for her unique look at Tibetan Buddhism. A dynamic speaker and the author of *A Course in Love* and *A Course in Life*, both of which have been translated into several languages, she is also a Unity minister in Shaker Heights, Ohio. Gattuso, whose spiritual path has taken her around the world to study with renowned spiritual leaders, lives in Ohio with her husband, David Alexander, and her two dogs.

He never came. It was sad. There was an empty place at the table and an empty place in our hearts that only he could fill. He still hasn't returned to the family, but our prayers continue without ceasing, and we have received a message that he is seeking personal help. That is an answer to our prayers for his well-being.

The gift of the sweater and invitation didn't bring him home for Christmas, but as I have heard the Dalai Lama teach many times: our prayers and spiritual practices for others may never show us a change in them, but they will always bring about a change in us.

Giving a gift to someone who has thrown you out of their heart cannot be done with any expectation of changed behavior on their part. It can only be done out of your own generous desire to show love, remembrance and caring.

MINDFULNESS, THE SECOND PERFECTION

This Perfection contains aspects that are medicine for the malaise of our times:

- Protecting all life—human, animal and plant. This means having a green consciousness and becoming aware of how all our actions impact Mother Earth, along with animals, pets and people.
- Preventing the exploitation of anyone. This means that when we see injustices, we do something about it.
- Protecting children and adults from sexual abuse. Again, action is required whenever we are made aware of such activity. During the holidays I was in a busy store waiting to be waited on when a mother across the counter completely lost her temper and began beating on her five- or six-year-old son, who obviously was annoying her. The other customers, the clerk and I stood in stunned silence. In such situations I am often at a loss as to what